Margaret Reynolds
February 5, 1925

LIBRARY IDEALS

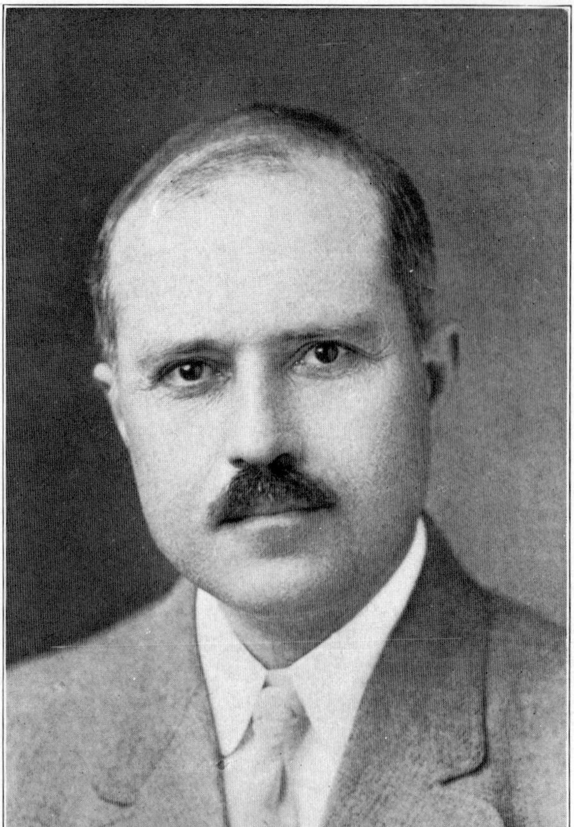

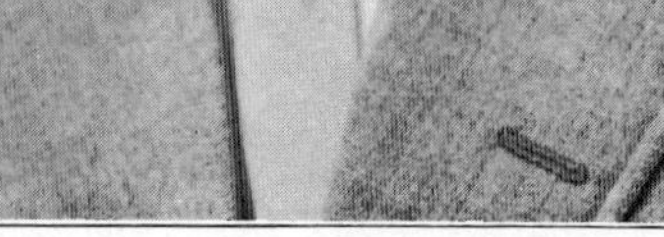

LIBRARY IDEALS

BY

HENRY E. LEGLER

Compiled and Edited by His Son,

HENRY M. LEGLER.

CHICAGO : : LONDON
THE OPEN COURT PUBLISHING COMPANY
1918

COPYRIGHT BY
THE OPEN COURT PUBLISHING COMPANY
1918

PRINTED IN THE UNITED STATES OF AMERICA

CONTENTS

Preface	VII
The Problem of the Cities	1
Certain Phases of Library Extension	10
Next Steps	21
The World of Print and the World's Work	36
Library Work With Children	57
Traveling Libraries	64
Administration of Library Funds	73

PREFACE

WISCONSIN, a true cradle of freedom and successful government, has fostered several librarians who were true humanists. Dr. Peckham was one. Dr. Thwaites was another. Henry E. Legler was unlike either of these, but greater than either in his continued and unabated activity for the good of the people.

Once, on being complimented for his splendid work in natural history and his persistence in the pursuit of scientific facts, Dr. Peckham remarked: "Oh, yes, but the facts have no value in themselves. They merely build up the groundwork of the ideas, and help you climb to the point of view where the deeper aspects of the subject spread out before you like a landscape beneath a mountain-top."

Mr. Legler's activity in behalf of libraries will support the same explanation. He seemed always immersed in detail, always planning some movement and carrying it into effect by his peculiar, dynamic persistence. But he who observed the man kindly and closely cannot have failed to have noticed that there was a distinct *Beyond* illumining and overshadowing it all. There was a dream to come true, a vision to be unfolded. The dream and vision were in the man's speech and eye. He lived under a prophecy.

It is not for us to estimate whether this prophecy became fulfilled in his life as one of us. But it is our privilege to confess that it brought to us the things which Europeans have designated as "culture" and which really is enlightenment. Thus it is that many of Mr. Legler's associates and friends will recollect with gratitude that some gave them knowledge, and others gave them opportunities, but it was for Mr. Legler to illumine their knowledge and opportunity with the live spark of inspiration.

The dream was in his eye, inspiration was in his speech and manner. Library work was the means in his power of making his fellow-men ever more free and happy, ever more master of themselves, ever more capable of being guided, not by fear and never by prejudice, but by a live responsibility to the spirit within them. Personally, though a most assiduous worker at his official desk in Milwaukee, Madison or Chicago, he always thought of escaping and of seeking some quiet spot in the wilderness—where, doubtless, he hoped to view his work from *above*. How many librarians nowadays have such a hope?

Of his method with the men and women of his age many of us will retain unforgettable memories. He was prompt, precise, perhaps even brief, but invariably gracious. His Italian ancestry told in the inimitable grace he unfolded to kindred spirits in confidence. We never were in doubt of the things he admired and fostered. We never felt there were hidden recesses of doubt and perplexity behind his sympathies. His grace of manner never was marred by contact with less enlightened surroundings. It is inimitable and unforgettable how he would pause in the midst of some matter of the moment, to plunge into some subject which he knew would interest and benefit the other person. And how grateful he was to strike a vein of gold in a seemingly unpromising human ore!

Secretary of the Milwaukee Board of Education, and Secretary of the Wisconsin Free Library Commission, Mr. Legler was already well versed in official service when chosen Librarian of the Chicago Public Library. He had declined several offers of important posts before that time, because the work he would give called for perfect freedom to work out the problems as he saw them. Wisconsin had given him this freedom. Chicago promised it—and kept her promise. There was sufficient prestige within the Chicago Public Library to warrant respect for, and liberal support of, its work, but the public estimate of this prestige was lacking. Other large cities possess this estimate in varying degree. Chicago—not its library—had fallen behind.

The effect of Mr. Legler's presence in Chicago has been most fortunate for all concerned. He took his place in public affairs naturally and effectively. The library's prestige grew in public recognition as the work of himself and his associates progressed. He gave all—and they accepted all, naturally and easily. But the giving and taking required all his bodily strength. He knew that an easier life was possible, but his humanity could not accept the easier form, and so the strength gave out.

But the spirit remains. Mr. Legler gave valuable contributions to historical investigation and to literary criticism, and he has published notable contributions to the elucidation of American forms of life., His contributions to library science and the art of books have been in part collected in the volume herewith presented. The main purpose in collecting them in the present form is to convey their purposes to the friends who like to remember the mind out of which they grew—and to perpetuate to others a memory of that burning zeal, that aspiring enthusiasm, that radical idealism, which animated Mr. Legler in choosing the library as the place where true humanism may be fostered and American enlightenment may flourish.

"Whatever began in the course of time—if of the Spirit of Truth and Love, it will be in time completed."

J. Christian Bay.

THE PROBLEM OF THE CITIES

UNCLE SAM'S last tabulation of his people holds within its maze of figures a basis for prophecy, as well as a summary of the present, and a comparison with the past. For those who are concerned with the making of an intelligent citizenship, perhaps the striking and significant fact is not the marvelous industrial development of the country, but rather the amazing growth of the cities. It needs no searching analysis to give emphasis to the sinister elements which are embodied in this bare statement. It means an approach to that critical period in the history of popular government when wise leadership and extension of education alone can serve to avert threatened disruption. Upon the people who are near to the soil will devolve the task of holding in balance the restless and turbulent elements which now make up so large a proportion of the dwellers in cities.

The modern growth of the city, with all that this movement in population implies, must be reckoned with everywhere. Greater New York has a population exceeding that of any state in the Union except its own. Chicago has within its city limits more people than any of forty states. The ten leading cities comprise together one-eighth of the total population of the United States. If New York City and Chicago and their conditions are extreme manifestations, it must be taken into account that in perhaps not to exceed a quarter and at most a half century, this growth cityward will be duplicated in every section of the United States. There are now 58 cities in the United States each counting more than 100,000 population, eight of them in excess of half a million each; there are 180 cities more each counting from 25,000 to 100,000 inhabitants.

It is hard to realize the rate of urban growth. In spite of the opening of vast tracts of land to be had almost for the asking, the total town population has multiplied in the last hundred years from 3 to approximately 50 per cent.

For the third or fourth time, the city is becoming the dominant factor in the world's history. The city-states of Greece rose and fell. Some of them became spoils of conquerors, others wasted from internal causes. Corinth once exercised sovereignty of the seas, but half a million of her population were slaves. When destroyed by the Carthaginians, Agrigentum was said to number two millions of people.

Genoa, Venice, the cities of the Hanseatic league, played their brief part in the commercial supremacy of their day. Rome once possessed a population of one million and a quarter, but though circled by beautiful villas and gardens, the common people lived congested in buildings whose floors and apartments were divided among numerous families. Famous writers have told us of the splendor and size of hundred-gated Thebes and Babylon and Antioch and Ephesus. But if there was splendor, there was vice; there was magnificence, but there dwelt squalor as well. Beauty and opulence fattening on human misery could not withstand famine, pestilence, and vice. The glories of the cities on the Nile, the Euphrates, and the Tiber are but a memory. And unless in the civic life of the modern city there is introduced an element that shall embrace the common good, perhaps Macaulay's oft-cited description of the New Zealander standing on the wreck of London bridge surveying the ruins of St. Paul's may yet become historic instead of merely prophetic.

It is perhaps but one of many evidences of the restlessness of the day that the lure of the city beckons with attraction inescapable to the youth of the countryside. Young men and young women who yield to the fascination find too late that they have sought Dead Sea Fruit,

> "Which charms the eye
> But turns to ashes on the lips."

The refuges and jails and lazarets and foul places of the great cities are filled with the derelicts of humanity who in less hectic atmosphere might have led lives of usefulness and contentment. Much has been done to give the life in the rural regions attractiveness and comfort; much more remains to be done, and particularly in supplying educational advantages, if the young men and women are to be made to feel that their opportunities are no less than those to be secured in larger cities of pulsing life. How wretchedly as yet this want has been met in most states, those charged with the supervision of educational activities can testify.

There are those who in the face of present-day economic conditions contend that any attempt to stop the great trek cityward must prove as futile as the back-to-the-soil movement has on the whole proved to be. Any such admission bodes but ill for the future of this land. It means that the number of men who feel an ownership in the land, in houses, in the government must decrease. And therein lies a danger not to be lightly disregarded.

Something of the dream and *Sehnsucht* that comes to the dreaming country boy, Robert Louis Stevenson has pictured with his wonder touch in his idyl of the miller's boy. Something, too, he has suggested in his ending of the story:

WILL O' THE MILL

"The mill where Will lived with his adopted parents stood in a falling valley between pine woods and great mountains. Above, hill after hill soared upwards until they soared out of the depths of the hardiest timber, and stood naked against the sky. Below, the valley grew ever steeper and steeper, and at the same time widened out on either hand: and from an eminence beside the mill it was possible to see its whole length and away beyond it over a wide plain, where the river turned and shone, and moved on from city to city on its voyage towards the sea. All through the summer, traveling carriages came crawling up, or went plunging briskly downwards past the mill; and as it happened that the other side was very much easier of ascent, the path was not much frequented, except by people going in one direction; five-sixths were plunging briskly downwards and only one-sixth crawling up.

"Whither went all the tourists and pedlars with strange wares? Whither all the brisk barouches with servants in the dicky? Whither the water of the stream, ever coursing downward and ever renewed from above? Even the wind blew oftener down the valley and carried the dead leaves along with it in the fall. It seemed like a great conspiracy of things animate and inanimate, they all went downward, fleetly and gaily downward, posting downward to the unknown world, and only he, it seemed, remained behind, like a stock upon the wayside.

"From that day forward Will was full of new hopes and longings. Something kept tugging at his heartstrings; the running water carried his desires along with it as he dreamed over its fleeting surface; the wind, as it ran over innumerable tree-tops, hailed him with encouraging words; branches beckoned downward; the open road, as it shouldered round the angles and went turning and vanishing faster and faster down the valley, tortured him with its solicitations. He spent long whiles on the eminence, looking down the rivershed and abroad on the low flatlands and watched the clouds that traveled forth upon the sluggish wind and trailed their purple shadows on the plain; or, he would linger by the wayside, and follow the carriages with his eyes as they rattled downward by the river. It did not matter what it was; everything that went that way, were it cloud or carriage, bird, or brown water in the stream, he felt his heart flow out after it, in an ecstacy of longing.

"One day, when Will was about sixteen, a young man arrived at sunset to pass the night. He was a contented-looking fellow, with a jolly eye, and carried a knapsack. While dinner was preparing, he sat in the arbour to read a book; but as soon as he had begun to observe Will, the book was laid aside; he was plainly one of those who prefer living people to people made of ink and paper. Will, on his part, although he had not been much interested in the stranger at first sight, soon began to take a great deal of pleasure in his talk, which was full of good nature and good sense, and at last conceived a great respect for his character and wisdom. They sat far into the night; and Will opened his heart to the young man, and told him how he longed to leave the valley and what bright hopes he had connected with the cities of the plain. The young man whistled, and then broke into a smile.

" 'My young friend,' he remarked, 'you are a very curious little fellow, to be sure, and wish a great many things which you will never get. Why, you would feel quite ashamed if you knew how the little fellows in these fairy cities of yours are all after the same sort of nonsense, and keep breaking their hearts to get up into the mountains. And let me tell you, those who go down into the plains are a very short while there before they wish themselves heartily back again. The air is not so light or so pure; nor is the sun any brighter. As for the beautiful men and women, you would see many of them in rags and many of them deformed; and a city is a hard place for people who are poor and sensitive.'

" 'You must think me very simple,' answered Will. 'Although I have never been out of this valley, believe me, I have used my eyes. I do not expect to find all things right in your cities. That is not what troubles me; it might have been that once upon a time; but although I live here always, I have asked many questions and learned a great deal in these last years, and certainly enough to cure me of my old fancies. But you would not have me die and not see all that is to be seen, and do all that a man can do, let it be good or evil?

You would not have me spend all my days between this road here and the river, and not so much as make a motion to be up and live my life? I would rather die out of hand,' he cried, 'than linger on as I am doing.'

" 'Thousands of people,' said the young man, 'live and die like you, and are none the less happy.'

" 'Ah!' said Will, 'if there are thousands who would like, why should not one of them have my place?'

"It was quite dark; there was a hanging lamp in the arbour which lit up the table and the faces of the speakers; and along the arch the leaves upon the trellis stood out illuminated against the bright sky, a pattern of transparent green upon a dusky purple. The young man rose, and, taking Will by the arm, led him out under the open heavens.

" 'Did you ever look at the stars?' he asked, pointing upwards.

" 'Often and often,' answered Will.

" 'And do you know what they are?'

" 'I have fancied many things.'

" 'They are worlds like ours,' said the young man. 'Some of them less; many of them a million times greater; and some of the least sparkles that you see are not only worlds, but whole clusters of worlds turning about each other in the midst of space.'

"Will hung his head a little, and then raised it once more to heaven. The stars seemed to expand and emit a sharper brilliancy; and as he kept turning his eyes higher and higher, they seemed to increase in multitude under his gaze. * * *

"Will went to and fro minding his wayside inn, until the snow began to thicken on his head. His heart was young and vigorous, and if his pulses kept a sober time, they still beat strong and steady in his wrists. He stooped a little, but his step was firm, and his sinewy hands were reached out to all men with a friendly pressure. His talk was full of wise sayings. He had a taste for other people and other people had a taste for him. His views seemed whimsical to his neighbors, but his rough philosophy was often enough admired by learned people out of town and colleges. Indeed, he had a very noble old age, and grew daily better known; so that his fame was heard of in the cities of the plains. Many and many an invitation to be sure, he had, but nothing could tempt him from his upland valley. He would shake his head and smile with a deal of meaning: 'Fifty years ago you would have brought my heart into my mouth; and now you do not even tempt me.' "

There is a legend of how a flying party of wanderers encountered a very old man shod with iron. The old man asked them whither they were going; and they answered with one voice: "To the Eternal City!" He looked upon them gravely. "I have sought it," he said, "over the most part of the world. Three such pairs as I now carry on my feet have I worn out upon my pilgrimage, and now the fourth is growing slender underneath my steps." And he turned and went his own way alone, leaving them astonished.

In the effort to make rural life of equal attractiveness with city life, it must be admitted that educational opporunities have lagged behind. Those who, by compulsion or otherwise, have left school in early years, find in the cities today abundant opportunity for self-help in the public libraries, in night schools, and in other agencies; the same opportunities are not provided to any appreciable extent in the country regions.

In the present stage of educational development, there are today millions of young men and women who find in the public library the only open door through which they catch glimpses of opportunity beyond their own immediate domain. With all the limitations involved, this is a hopeful circumstance, for instances are plentiful where "the chance encounter with a book has marked the awakening of a life." One need not go to works of fiction to seek such stories, but in them may be found types which have been plucked from bits of real life. And in real life they could be multiplied a thousand times. Perhaps you recall the household of the Tullivers' when misfortune came upon it, and the change which a few well-thumbed volumes made in one of its members:

"The new life was terrible to Maggie—Maggie with her strange dreams, with her hunger for love. Her father no longer stroked her hair as he used to do when she sat down in her low stool beside him at night, though he was more dependent on her than ever. Tom, weary and full of his new business ambitions, did not respond to her caresses. The poor mother remained hopelessly bewildered under the blow that had fallen on her placid existence.

"The girl fell back on the meagre remnant of books that had been left by the creditors. She studied Virgil and Euclid and spent her days in the fields with the Latin dictionary and Tom's thumbed schoolbooks. One day she chanced on a worn copy of Thomas á Kempis, and she pushed her heavy hair back from her sad brow as if to see a sudden vision more clearly. That chronicle of a solitary, hidden anguish, struggle, faith and triumph came to her in her need and filled her heart with the writer's fervor of renunciation.

"Her new inward life shone out in her face with a tender, soft light that mingled itself as added loveliness with the enriched color and outline of her blossoming youth. Maggie was beginning to show a queenly head above her old frocks, and her mother felt the change with a puzzled, dim wonder that the once 'contrary' and ugly child should be 'growing up so good.'"

The higher life of the citizen has received too little attention, and the lower and baser life seems to have absorbed all the sympathy and care of the authorities. But we have touched the fringe of better days, and soon no municipality or local governing body will be considered complete unless it has under its administration a library and a museum, as well as a workhouse, a prison, and the preserves of law and order. It is for the provision for this higher national life that this plea is made, and upon municipalities is earnestly urged the need of giving the fullest and best attention to this question. The fact should be emphasized that the municipality can do for the people in the way of libraries and museums what cannot possibly be done by private enterprise. It may be unhesitatingly asserted that in fullest usefulness, economical management, and best value for money invested, the existing rate-supported libraries are far in advance of the private institutions of this nature.

It is some forty years since Carlyle asked the question, "Why is there not a Majesty's library in every county town? There is a Majesty's gaol and gallows in every one," and it is as long since the Public Libraries Act was passed, and yet the lack of libraries is still one of the most startling deficiencies in these islands. We have given the people ever greater and greater political power, but they displayed no marked inclination to benefit themselves by means of books or other means of culture.

"We must now educate our masters," said Mr. Lowe when the Reform Bill of 1867 was passed. He was quite right, for the said masters were by no means quick to educate themselves, and the number of public libraries which they consented to establish for three years after 1867 was about ten.

Then came Mr. Forster's Education Act, and great things were expected of it. Now that everybody was to be taught his letters, everybody would surely want books to read also. What, indeed, would be the good of teaching people to read at all unless they were also to have a supply of good books? You might as well teach a man the use of his knife and fork and then not give him any meat.

Public libraries are the natural and legitimate outcome of compulsory education.

CERTAIN PHASES OF LIBRARY EXTENSION[1]

DREAMING of Utopia, an English writer of romance evolved a plan for a people's palace, centering under one roof the pleasures and the interests and the hopes of democracy. Far away, if not improbable, as seemed the fruition of his dream, he lived to see prophecy merge in realization. Were this lover of mankind still living, he would know that his concept, though he saw it carried into being, had not permanence in the form he gave it. Ideals cannot be bounded by the narrow confines of four walls. And yet he had the vision of the seer, for that which he pictured in local form with definite limitations has, in a direction little dreamed of then, assumed form and substance in a great world movement. Not only in great hives of industry, where thousands congregate in daily toil, but in the small industrial hamlets and in the rural towns that dot the land lie the possibilities for many such palaces of the people, and in many—very many—of such communities today exist the beginnings that will combine and cement their many-sided interests.

This great world movement which is gathering accelerated momentum with its own marvelous growth, we call library extension. That term is perhaps sufficiently descriptive, though it gives name rather to the

[1] Address delivered on behalf League of Library Commissions, Asheville Conference A. L. A., May 27, 1907.

means used than to the results sought to be achieved. For certainly its underlying principle is of the very essence of democracy. There is no other governmental enterprise—not excepting the public schools—that so epitomizes the spirit of democracy. For democracy in its highest manifestation is not that equality that puts mediocrity and idleness on the same level with talent and genius and thrift, but that equality which gives *all* members of society an equal opportunity in life—that yields to no individual as a birthright chances denied to his fellow. And surely if there is any institution that represents this fundamental principle and carries out a policy in consonance, it is the public library. Neither condition nor place of birth, nor age, nor sex, nor social position, serves as bar of exclusion from this house of the open door, of the cordial welcome, of the sympathetic aid freely rendered. In myriad ways not dreamed of at its inception, library extension has sought channels of usefulness to reach all the people. The traveling library in rural regions, the branch stations in congested centers of population, the children's room, the department of technology, are a few of these—to mention the ones which occur most readily to mind.

But these allied agencies do but touch the edge of opportunity. The immediate concern of those engaged in library extension must be with the forces reaching the adult population, and especially the young men and women engaged in industrial pursuits. For the mission of the public library is two-fold—an aid to material progress of the individual and a cultural influence in the community through the individual. Perhaps it may be said more accurately that the one mission is essential to give scope for the second. For, first of all, man must needs minister to his physical wants. Before there can be intellectual expansion and cultural development, there must be leisure, or at least conditions that free the mind from anxious care for the morrow. So the social structure after all must rest upon a bread-and-butter foundation. It follows as a logical conclusion that society as a whole cannot reach a high stage of development until all its individual members are surrounded with conditions that permit the highest self-development. Until a better agency shall be found, it is the public library which must serve this need. And therein lies the most potent reason for the extension of its work into every field, whether intimately or remotely affiliated, which can bring about these purposes. Its work with children is largely important to the extent that habits are formed and facility acquired in methods that shall be utilized in years succeeding school life. But its great problem is that of adult education. What an enormous field still lies untilled, we learn with startling emphasis from figures compiled by the government. Despite the fact that provision is made by state and municipality to give to every individual absolutely without cost an education embracing sixteen years of life, there are retarding circumstances that prevent all but a mere fraction of the population from enjoying these advantages in full measure.

To quote a summary printed last year, "in the United States 16,511,024 were receiving elementary education during the year 1902-03; only 776,635 attained to a secondary education, and only 251,819 to the higher education of the colleges, technical schools, etc. Stated in simpler terms, this means that in the United States for one person who receives a higher education, or for three who receive the education of the secondary schools, there are sixty-five who receive only an elementary education, and that chiefly in the lowest grades of the elementary schools."

What gives further meaning to this statistical recital is the force of modern economic conditions. From an agricultural we are developing into a manufacturing people, with enormous influx from the rural into the urban communities. The tremendous expansion of our municipalities has brought new and important problems. Within the lifetime of men today a hundred cities have realized populations in excess of that which New York City had when they were boys. Vast numbers of immigrants differing radically in intelligence and in education from earlier comers are pouring into the country annually. It has been pointed out that some of the largest Irish, German and Bohemian cities in the world are located in the United States, not in their own countries. In one ward in the city of Chicago forty languages are spoken by persons who prattled at their mother's knee one or the other of them.

"The power of the public schools to assimilate different races to our own institutions, through the education given to the younger generation, is doubtless one of the most remarkable exhibitions of vitality that the world has ever seen," says Dr. John Dewey in an address on "The School as a Social Center." "But, after all, it leaves the older generation still untouched, and the assimilation of the younger can hardly be complete or certain as long as the homes of the parents remain comparatively unaffected. Social, economic and intellectual conditions are changing at a rate undreamed of in past history. Now, unless the agencies of instruction are kept running more or less parallel with these changes, a considerable body of men is bound to find itself without the training which will enable it to adapt itself to what is going on. It will be left stranded and become a burden for the community to carry. The youth at eighteen may be educated so as to be ready for the conditions which will meet him at nineteen; but he can hardly be prepared for those which are to confront him when he is forty-five. If he is ready for the latter when they come, it is because his own education has been keeping pace in the intermediate years."

And again: "The daily occupations and ordinary surroundings of life are much more in need of interpretation than ever they have been before. Life is getting so specialized, the divisions of labor are carried so far that nothing explains or interprets itself. The worker in a modern factory who is concerned with a fractional piece of a complex activity, presented to him only in a limited series of acts carried on with a distinct position of a machine, is typical of much in our entire social life. Unless the lives of a large part of our wage earners are to be left to their own barren meagerness, the community must see to it by some organized agency that they are instructed in the scientific foundation and social bearings of the things they see about them, and of the activities in which they are themselves engaging."

Now if those who come in such limited numbers from the colleges and universities, can keep step with the onward march of their fellows only by constantly adding to their educational equipment, what shall be said of that enormous army made up of conscripts from the ranks in the elementary schools?—the tender hands that drop the spelling book and seize the workman's dinner pail?

Thus we establish the duty of the state to its citizenship in providing means for adult education. And herein lies a great opportunity for library extension— not, indeed, in seeking to supplant agencies already existent; not in creating new ones that will parallel others, but in supplementing their work where such educational agencies do exist, in supplying channels for their activities through its own greater facilities for reaching the masses. Important as are the public museum, the public art gallery, the popular lecture or lyceum feature, the public debate associated with or incorporated in the library, of as far-reaching importance is another and newer allied agency developed in university extension. The response which has come in establishing correspondence study as part of modern university extension is of tremendous significance. The enrollment in correspondence schools of a million grown-up men and women eager to continue their education, and willing to expend more than fifty million dollars a year in furtherance of that desire, is a factor that challenges attention. It is a new expression of an old impulse. Eighty years ago the working people and artisan classes of Great Britain took part in a similar movement. Its beginning was prompted by a wish for technical instruction. Soon these mechanics' institutes grew into social institutions, with collections of books as a secondary interest. The institutes increased enormously in number, until through their medium more than a million volumes a year were circulated. Charles Knight issued his penny encyclopedia, Robert and William Chambers led the way for inexpensive books, the Society for the Diffusion of Knowledge came into existence. Industrial England was for the time being the workshop of the world. And in the later university extension movement which, along new lines, is to make of universities having a state foundation really the instrument of the state for the good of all the people in place of the few, the libraries have a great opportunity to become an important factor. Millions of the adult population will thus be given an opportunity to bring out in its best form whatever of talent and of intellectual gift they may possess. From a private letter written by Professor McConachie, of the University of Wisconsin, who has charge of the correspondence study in the department of science, are taken the following extracts: "Old ways of teaching are breaking down. Library study and written exercises are re-enforcing classroom recitations and lectures. Each pupil of a term course studies one or two prescribed texts, reads and reports in detail a minimum of eight or nine hundred pages in a choice shelf collection of library books, takes and submits notes, writes brief themes and prepares for weekly quizzes wherein the members of his class section helpfully interchange ideas and information. The post-office is the medium for extension from the university to a vaster body of students everywhere throughout the state. The same materials—books, periodicals, newspapers, and official documents,—that the student of politics uses under the personal oversight of the university instructor, are scattered in vast abundance everywhere. The state is one great library. The largest single collection is paltry beside this magnificent and ever-increasing supply of political literature that permeates every hamlet. Civic intelligence has thriven upon the mere haphazard and desultory reading of the people. Correspondence studies will put their scattered material into shape for them and systematize their use thereof." The library and the university may serve the citizen by giving unity and direction to his reading, helping him to hitherto hidden worth and meaning in the humblest literary material at his hand, by quickening his interest alike in the offices, institutions and activities that lie nearest to his daily life and in his world-wide relationship with his fellowmen. For the citizen on the farm, at the desk, or in the factory, they point the way out of vague realizations into distinct and definite command of his political self, offer refreshing change from the narrowing viewpoint of individual interest, to the broadening viewpoint of his town or state or country, and lead on to far international vistas of world-wide life and destiny.

Society has an interest in this beyond the rights of the individual. The greatest waste to society is not

PHASES OF LIBRARY EXTENSION 17

that which comes from improvidence, but from undeveloped or unused opportunity. So it becomes the duty of every community to make its contribution to the world, whether it be in the realm of invention, scientific discovery, or literature. And how is this to be done if genius and talent are allowed to die unborn for lack of opportunity to grow? Wonderful as has been the progress of the world's knowledge during the last century of scientific research, who will venture to say that it constitutes more than a fraction of what might have been if all the genius that remained dormant and unproductive could have been utilized? From what we know of isolated instances where mere chance has saved to the world great forces that make for the progress of humanity, we can infer what might have been realized, under happier conditions. Every librarian of experience, every administrator of traveling libraries, will recall such instances. One boy comes upon the right book, and the current of his life is changed; another reads a volume, and in his brain germinates the seed that blossoms into a great invention; in a chance hour of reading, a third finds in a page, a phrase, a word, the inspiration whose expression sets aflame the world. A master pen has vividly described the process:[2]

"Most of us who turn to any subject with love remember some morning or evening hour when we got on a high stool to reach down an untried volume. * * * When hot from play he would toss himself in a corner, and in five minutes be deep in any sort of book that he could lay his hands on; if it were Rasselas or Gulliver, so much the better, but Bailey's Dictionary would do, or the Bible with the Apocrypha in it. Something he must read when he was not riding the pony, or running and hunting, or listening to the talk of men. * * * But, one vacation, a wet day sent him to the small home library to hunt once more for a book which might have some

[2] George Eliot, "Middlemarch."

freshness for him. In vain! unless, indeed, he first took down a dusty row of volumes with gray-paper backs and dingy labels—the volumes of an old encyclopedia which he had never disturbed. It would at least be a novelty to disturb them. They were on the highest shelf, and he stood on a chair to get them down; but he opened the volume which he took first from the shelf; somehow one is apt to read in a makeshift attitude just where it might seem inconvenient to do so. The page he opened on was under the head of Anatomy, and the first passage that drew his eyes was on the valves of the heart. He was not much acquainted with valves of any sort, but he knew that valvæ were folding doors, and through this crevice came a sudden light startling him with his first vivid notion of finely-adjusted mechanism in the human frame. A liberal education had, of course, left him free to read the indecent passages in the school classics, but beyond a general sense of secrecy and obscenity in connection with his internal structure, had left his imagination quite unbiased, so that for anything he knew his brains lay in small bags at his temples, and he had no more thought of representing to himself how his blood circulated than how paper served instead of gold. But the moment of vocation had come, and before he got down from his chair the world was made new to him by a presentiment of endless processes filling the vast spaces planked out of his sight by that wordy ignorance which he had supposed to be knowledge. From that hour he felt the growth of an intellectual passion."

And in this wise the world gained a great physician.

All this may be said without disparagement to that phase of library usefulness which may be termed the recreative. There has been undue and unreasoning criticism of the library tendency to minister to the novel-reading habit. Many good people are inclined to decry the public library because not all its patrons confine their loans to books dealing with science, or with useful arts. In their judgment it is not the legitimate function of the public library to meet the public demand for fiction. These same good people would hardly urge that the freedom of the public parks should be limited to those who wish to make botanical studies. The pure joy in growing things and fresh air and the song of uncaged birds, needs no knowledge of scientific terms in botany and ornithology. These privileges are promotive of the physical well-being of the people; correspondingly, healthy mental stimulus is to be found in "a sparkling and sprightly story which may be read in an hour and which will leave the reader with a good conscience and a sense of cheerfulness." Our own good friend, Mr. John Cotton Dana, has admirably epitomized the underlying philosophy:

"A good story has created many an oasis in many an otherwise arid life. Many-sidedness of interest makes for good morals, and millions of our fellows step through the pages of a story book into a broader world than their nature and their circumstances ever permit them to visit. If anything is to stay the narrowing and hardening process which specialization of learning, specialization of inquiry and of industry and swift accumulation of wealth are setting up among us, it is a return to romance, poetry, imagination, fancy, and the general culture we are now taught to despise. Of all these the novel is a part; rather, in the novel are all of these. But a race may surely find springing up in itself a fresh love of romance, in the high sense of that word, which can keep it active, hopeful, ardent, progressive. Perhaps the novel is to be, in the next few decades, part of the outward manifestation of a new birth of this love of breadth and happiness."

There is, then, no limitation to the scope of library extension save that enforced by meagerness of resource and physical ability to do. In the proper affiliation and correlation of all these forces which have been enumerated and of others suggested by them, will develop that process whereby the social betterment that today seems but a dream will be brought into reality. The form this combination will assume need give us no concern—whether its local physical expression shall be as in Boston a group of buildings maintained as separate institutions; or as in Pittsburgh, a complete, related scheme of activities covered by one roof; as planned in Cleveland, a civic center with the public library giving it character and substance; or as in New York, where many institutions, remotely located but intimately associated, work toward a common end. Many roads may lead to a common center. Which one the wayfarer chooses is a matter of mere personal preference and of no importance, so that he wends his way steadily onwards towards the object of his attainment. In the evolution of these uplifting processes, the book shall stand as symbol, as the printed page shall serve as instrument.

NEXT STEPS[1]

OF ALL human interests that pertain to intellectual improvement—social evolution, scientific achievement, educational progress, governmental advance, or humanitarian endeavor, none has seemed too unimportant for consideration by library workers. Librarians have sought to identify their work with them all, to achieve contact with every individual, with groups of individuals and with communities as a whole. If intelligent method has sometimes seemed lacking, the enthusiasm and the self-denial of the missionary have been given in unstinted measure. To the home and to the mart, to the school and to the playground, to the workshop and to the laboratory, they have brought —whether asked or unsought—the best at their command.

Not out of abundance has the library attempted so much in such diverse places. Its meager resources have been spread over such vast fields that in spots the substance has seemed tenuous and transparent. Most insufficient, and perhaps least successful thus far, but suggesting the most important function of library activity and presaging its most significant development, is that branch of service associated with grammar and secondary schools. Here lies the most fertile field for

[1] Read before the New York Library Association at Haines Falls, Sept. 28, 1915.

strong, vigorous, fruitful energizing of such forces as the library possesses.

Curiously enough, a perception of values which inhere in the associated and co-ordinated efforts of school and library has not, as yet, dawned upon school men to any appreciable degree. Here and there, indeed, a vibrant voice has demanded the joining of effort for practical ends, but the teaching folk as a whole remain impervious to possibilities even when sensible of the need. Nearly four centuries ago, Martin Luther noted the possibilities of the library as an educational adjunct and necessity, and urged the founding of public libraries for the preservation and encouragement of learning.[2]

"No cost nor pains," he urged in the concluding pages of his letter to the mayors of Germany, "should be spared to procure good libraries in suitable buildings, especially in the large cities which are able to afford it."

From his day to ours there appears in printed works on education—whether general or dealing with specialized phases—no recurrent note amplifying this suggestion, except a few casual fugitive references in less than a dozen recent publications, and two treatises that recognize the importance of the subject with some fulness of treatment. Perhaps this sweeping characterization of stolid school-room self-sufficiency should be modified by crediting to Horace Mann a vision that scarcely survived his passing. A historian of educational influences informs us that in Mr. Mann's work for teachers two aspects are apparent—one dealing with preparation, the other with method. Through his labors normal schools became a component part of our school system, and institutes were started for the spe-

[2] Painter. History of Education.

cial training of teachers. Furthermore, he made apparent the value of libraries as school adjuncts, and brought about their establishment. And similarly in backwoods Wisconsin, three-quarters of a century ago, Lyman Draper sought to interest the teaching forces there. His report printed in the 50's—now rare and difficult to procure—is a grouping of opinions, prophetic but yet unrealized, expressed by eminent men of the day as foreshadowing a relationship of school and library.

A careful examination of fifty average books on education issued since 1870 yields but scant encouragement to those who seek association of school and library. Six of the fifty writers give at least passing consideration to the subject. Two cyclopedias of education recognize the importance of the subject.[3]

Forty-two books issued between the years mentioned, and about equally divided between the decades represented are wholly barren of such mention. On the other hand, two are notable for vital grasp and broad treatment—G. Stanley Hall's chapters in the second volume of his *"Educational Problems,"* and Hugo Müsterberg's chapter in *"The Americans."*

Significant of present-day conditions is the testimony of a teacher, who, addressing a library gathering, said:[4]

"In days gone by we carried on the school without libraries—we could do this as well as not because education meant *learning by rote;* text-book learning alone.

---

[3] One devotes thereto a column and a half of 1736 columns in the volume, and the other devotes 37 columns to the subject of the 1480 columns contained in one of the five volumes of the work.

[4] *Library Journal.*

"This is, to my mind, the most important thing I have to say to you—we do not yet know you and our need for you.

"In our school lives as children, in our normal training and later in our actual teaching we have not had you, and we do not yet realize your resources.

To get this matter before you definitely, pardon my using my own case as illustration.

"From beginning to end of my common school education—from the first grade through eighth—I never saw a school or a public library. We had none, though I lived in a good-sized city in the Middle West. I learned what the text-book told me; no supplementary reading (or rarely), no pictures, no objects. My training in reading and literature consisted in learning to keep my toes on a crack and my voice from falling on a question mark!

"In high school I had very little but the regular text. Again memory work was the test. I remember well a boy who was my ideal. He learned his geography word for word and so recited it. If he sneezed or a door slammed and his flow of words (I use words advisedly) was interrupted, he had to begin again. He was the show pupil in our class.

"In college our instructors in science performed all the experiments for us while we looked on. When we went to the library we spoke to the librarian through a wire netting, and in our company manners asked for a book.

"In the normal school which I attended there was a so-called children's library, but the books were all text-books, and we were not taught how to help the children to use them. We had literature, but it was all about Hamlet's being or not being mad; none of it was taught in a way to make it a tool for the elementary teacher.

"After all this I began teaching, with no knowledge of the resources of a library as an aid to either teacher or child, and I felt no need for such aid. What is true of me is true of thousands of other teachers.

"You must make us feel our need for you. You must, if you please, intrude yourselves upon our notice. Generations of teachers who have worshipped at the shrine of the text-book can in no other way be reached.

"The ideals of education today are broader, our needs are greater, and you have the material to help us to realize our needs."

In the relatively few instances where co-operation between school and library administration has led to installation of modern library equipment in elementary schools, the difficulties have been experienced which are usual when afterthought supplies what forethought neglects to include. Quarters are ordinarily unsuitable and insufficient. Adequate provision should be made when school buildings are planned, for library quarters that are ample as to size and strategic as to location, instead of depending for space upon a room or enlarged closet not otherwise utilized, for library placement. Perhaps it is too optimistic to hope for a change soon in the inconceivably stupid architecture and design of school buildings, despite a few recent striking examples to the contrary.

As now financed, no public library system can undertake to administer a branch library in every grade school building within its jurisdiction. For school service on such a liberal scale there would be required in the city of New York at least $4,300,000 for equipment and at least $537,000 annually for current maintenance; in Chicago, $2,350,000 for initial equipment and $294,000 annually for maintenance; in other cities, correspondingly large expenditures. However, in most of the major cities of the United States, it is entirely feasible to make a reasonable beginning by introducing some features of the work not now attempted, or tried in such meagre fashion as to be useless and disheartening. As there are in many places traveling school libraries, so there may well be added traveling school librarians. It is imperative that for this service there must be sought a type of teacher-librarian capable by reason of natural ability and education to command the confidence of the teaching corps as a counselor, and of the student body as a friendly element in the school, disassociated from the thought of book use based on compulsion. A teacher-librarian so qualified could exert an important influence in shaping the future of the children.

In his inimitable, whimsical fashion, Bernard Shaw brings out with sympathy and humor something of this spirit of compulsion which schools typify:

"There is, on the whole, nothing on earth intended for innocent people so horrible as a school. To begin with, it is a prison. But it is in some respects more cruel than a prison. In a prison, for instance, you are not forced to read books written by the warders and the governor (who, of course, would not be warders and governors if they could write readable books), and are therefore beaten or otherwise tormented if you cannot remember their utterly unmemorable contents. In the prison you are not forced to sit listening to turnkeys discoursing without charm or interest on subjects that they don't understand and don't care about, and are therefore incapable of making you understand or care about. In a prison they may torture your body; but they do not torture your brains; and they protect you against violence and outrage from your fellow prisoners. In a school you have none of these advantages. With the world's book-shelves loaded with fascinating and inspired books—the very manna sent down from heaven to feed your souls—you are forced to read a hideous imposture called a school book, written by a man who cannot write; a book from which no human being can learn anything; a book which, though you may decipher it, you cannot in any fruitful sense read, though the enforced attempt will make you loathe the sight of a book all the rest of your life. It is a ghastly business, quite beyond words, this schooling."

The late Professor Norton is credited[5] with the statement that a taste for literature is a result of cultivation more often than a gift of nature, and that the years of the elementary school seem to be the time in which the taste takes deepest root. Dr. Scott Nearing[6] points out that the old education presupposed an average child and then prepared a course of study which would fit his needs. The new education, he contends, recognizes the absurdity of averaging unlike quantities, and accepts the ultimate truth that each child is an individual, differing in needs, capacity, outlook, energy, and enthusiasm from every other child. An arithmetic average can be struck, but when it is applied to children it is a hypothetical and not a real quantity. There is not, and never will be, an average child; hence, a school system planned to meet the needs of the average child fits the needs of no child at all.

Rightly directed, library influences in elementary schools would modify the machine-like formula giving to all children alike at the same time the same mental food to eat and the same moral garb to wear. As Dr. Bird T. Baldwin notes in his ingenious statement of the five ages of childhood, school children are inevitably different; even when children are born on the same day, the chances that they will grow physically, mentally and morally at exactly the same rate, and will

[5]Lowe. Literature for Children.

[6]Nearing, Scott. The New Education.

make exactly the same progress in school, are remote indeed.

A teacher-librarian having special aptitude for the post could render service of inestimable value to teachers as well as to their pupils, in becoming the active medium between public school and public library. By securing the right books from the library for home reading, by providing picture material and reference sources for class room use, by conducting story hours and reading clubs, by giving instruction in the use of the library and the keys that open books, by giving stimulus to the ambitions and capacities of individual pupils, by intimate co-operation with the work of vocational guidance, the librarian would prove her worth. Nor would the least useful function of the school libraries be that of an evening study place for those tens of thousands of children whose home conditions absolutely preclude thought of, or opportunity for, study out of school hours.

It may be contended that these services are provided by branch libraries and their juvenile departments. What are the facts? Early in the present month twenty million boys and girls went more or less willingly to school. Our consolidated library statistics show that considerably less than one million of them use our public libraries. Despite our imposing figures of circulation, we reach but 5 per cent of the juvenile population.

If there are urgent reasons for increased library effort in connection with grade schools, these apply with multiplied force as to high schools. Here, indeed, the deterrent factor of enormous and prohibitive cost would not obtain, because they are fewer in number; and in proportion to total cost of maintenance, the added percentage of cost would be comparatively small. There are in the United States 8,300 high schools with a four-year course, and 3,250 carrying a three-year course. In every one of the 11,500 high schools there should be a well-equipped and well-administered library. Preferably, those that are located in cities where there are strong public libraries should be conducted as branches of the local public library. Such management would assure better administration. School management would imperil in many instances the selection of librarians fitted for the task. Too often, as experience has demonstrated, the governing body would assign to the post derelict teachers unfitted by reason of age or physical handicap, and unfortunate deficiencies in other respects. On the other hand, public library authorities must recognize more tangibly than they do now that high school librarians must possess not only library training in the machinery of routine performance, but also university education, teaching experience, and qualifications of personality and temperament that will place them on a level with other members of the faculty.

In the high schools we find the sifted grain of the elementary schools. It is there that the potential qualities of originality and genius which will later make their impress upon the course of industry and government must be quickened and given direction. More and more it is coming to be realized that to grasp without failure the complexities of modern life native intelligence no longer suffices.

Intelligence must be sharpened by education and given power by experience. The self-made man who achieved success untaught, unlettered, and unaided save by his own efforts of hand and brain, has become a legendary hero. Appreciation of changed conditions may be found in the records of increased attendance in the high schools. That increase has been at a greater rate than that of the population. In 1890 there were but 59 pupils for every ten thousand inhabitants; in 1895 there were 79; in 1900 there were 95; in 1910 there were 100; and now the number is considerably in excess, statistics for 1914 showing 117. Thus, in twenty-five years, the percentage of high school attendance has nearly doubled.

Again we find the school people without perception of the great value which a properly conducted library would bring to a high school. In his recently published book, *"The New Education,"* Dr. Scott Nearing describes an up-to-date high school:

"The modern high school," he says, "is housed in a building which contains, in addition to the regular classrooms, gymnasiums, a swimming tank, physics and chemical laboratories; cooking, sewing, and millinery rooms; woodworking, forge, and machine shops; drawing rooms; a music room; a room devoted to arts and crafts; and an assembly room. This arrangement of rooms presupposes Mr. Gilbert's plan of making the high school, like the community, an aggregation of every sort of people, doing every sort of work."

When some of the foremost leaders in education leave out of a list of desiderata for the high school what the universities have come to regard as the very heart of the institution—the library—is there marvel that the love of literature is being strangled in the schools? Required reading of classics, and the use of literary masterpieces for classroom dissection has taken away the pure joy of reading and made the study of literature a mere literary autopsy. Here is the testimony of a teacher who places herself on the witness stand:[7]

[7]Hodgson, Elizabeth. The Adolescent's Prejudice Against the Classics. *English Journal,* Sept., 1915.

"Sometimes the high school course works as a sort of vaccination to prevent their taking literature seriously.

"Most teachers of English have had at times the experience holding open a volume of Shakespeare with one hand, while with the other they waved some sort of scholastic rod over the head of a rebellious young modern. Though 'classics' are probably swallowed with less forcible feeding than grammar, spelling, and rhetoric, yet even those dilutable bits of literature that have been considered food for the gods of culture are gulped down wry-facedly by some barbarians. By judicious skimming and cramming they may perforce capture the irreducible minimum of scanty and fugitive facts about the masterpieces prescribed for their edification; but at the first safe moment they joyously forget them, and betake themselves to the cheaper theaters, the thrilling dailies, and the popular novelists.

"The truth is that literature teachers are devoted champions of a lost cause. Some of the dead authors appear to be so irrevocably dead that no amount of artificial respiration can put any breath of life into their works so far as the ordinary high school student is concerned.

"It would be enticingly easy to win over students to a course in journalism, modern magazines, and contemporary novels and dramas.

"We cannot expect to overcome all the narrowing and even vulgarizing influences that surround many of our young people; but at least we should improve their judgment enough to make them reject the cheapest, shallowest, and most distorted contemporary writings."

One chapter of Ernest Poole's story of *"The Har-*

bor" tells of his school experience. A passage from it is worth quoting:

"What a desert of knowledge it was back there. Our placid tolerance of the profs included the books they gave us. The history prof gave us ten books of collateral reading. Each book, if we could pledge our honor as gentlemen that we had read it, counted us five in examination. On the night before the examination I happened to enter the room of one of our football giants, and found him surrounded by five freshmen, all of whom were reading aloud. One was reading a book on Russia, another the life of Frederick the Great, a third was patiently droning forth Napoleon's war on Europe, while over on the window-seat the other two were racing through volumes one and two of Carlyle's French Revolution. The room was a perfect babel of sound. But the big man sat and smoked his pipe, his honor safe and the morrow secure. In later years, whatever might happen across the sea would find this fellow fully prepared, a wise, intelligent judge of the world, with a college education."

Into the atmosphere of the school must be introduced some element that will bring to the growing boys and girls a love of reading and a genuine desire for absorbing those vital forces of life which literature images. If we believe that the ultimate aim of education is that of the ultimate aim of life, there must be that attenion to the individual need which in the end makes for the uplifting of all. To that end the means must be wrought. If the school must deal perforce with groups rather than with units, the methods of the library adapt themselves to the converse plan of individual treatment. If the school narrows the pathway by compulsion, the library gives the joy of freedom unrestricted. Therein lies its potency, and therein does it make appeal not to the few elect, but to the many. And herein lies its greater service.

"Progress is
The law of life, man is not man as yet,
Nor shall I deem his object served, his end

> Attained, his genuine strength put fairly forth,
> While only here and there a star dispels
> The darkness, here and there a towering mind
> O'erlooks its prostrate fellows: when the host
> Is out at once to the despair of night,
> When all mankind alike is perfected,
> Equal in full-blown powers—then, not till then,
> I say, begins man's general infancy."

Wherefore this emphasis upon the school side of library work? Not, of course, at the expense of the service which is furnished to young and old in relief from the drab dullness of life, but parallel with it, must the library labor. For here lies its mission of permanent influences, and at no time has there been greater need.

Suddenly, the seemingly well-fortified pillars of civilization have crumbled. Confused, dismayed, disheartened, society witnesses rapid disintegration of foundations which centuries of patient endeavor have constructed. Science, thought to be the instrument of man's weal, has become the subtle and baleful agent of destruction. The racial hyphen, long looked upon as the symbol of cohesion, has become the sign of separation. The Christian nations of the earth are at each other's throats with a ferocity and malignity unparalleled. Under a flag which shelters ninety millions of individuals whose forebears peopled every land upon the habitable globe, and who seek to merge the best of their racial qualities in a common life that shall typify a new standard of civilization, must be wrought that miracle of human evolution which shall establish concord and good will between members of alien races dwelling together. To effect this it must be demonstrated that "assimilation is a matter of understanding and ideas, and not merely of manners and customs."

And so, despite the gloomy murk that now envelops the world, we must realize the need of beginning the reconstruction of our demolished ideals.

This is the day of readjustments. We must begin again, but we must begin at the point of beginning, with the plastic mind of youth. Happily, if not now, generations hence, the world may realize the poet's prophecy, and the hope it holds:

> "For no new sense puts forth in us but we
> Enter our fellow's lives thereby the more.
>
> And three great spirits with the spirit of man
> Go forth to do his bidding. One is free,
> And one is shackled, and the third, unbound,
> Halts yet a little with a broken chain
> Of antique workmanship, not wholly loosed,
> That dangles and impedes his forthright way.
> Unfettered, swift, hawk-eyed, implacable,
> The wonder-worker, Science, with his wand,
> Subdues an alien world to man's desires.
> And Art with wide imaginative wings
> Stands by, alert for flight, to bear his lord,
> Into the strange heart of that alien world
> Till he shall live in it as in himself
> And know its longing as he knows his own.
> Behind a little, where the shadows fall,
> Lingers Religion with deep-brooding eyes,
> Serene, impenetrable, transpicuous
> As the all-clear and all-mysterious sky,
> Biding her time to fuse into one act
> Those other twain, man's right hand and his left.
>
> For all the bonds shall be broken and rent in sunder,
> And the soul of man go free
> Forth with those three
> Into the lands of wonder;
> Like some undaunted youth,
> Afield in quest of truth,

Rejoicing in the road he journeys on
As much as in the hope of journey done.
And the road runs east, and the road runs west,
That his vagrant feet explore;
And he knows no haste and he knows no rest,
And every mile has a stranger zest
Then the miles he trod before;
And his heart leaps high in the nascent year
When he sees the purple buds appear:
For he knows, though the great black frost may blight
The hope of May in a single night,
That the spring, though it shrink back under the bark,
But bides its time somewhere in the dark—
Though it come not now to its blossoming,
By the thrill in his heart he knows the spring;
And the greater to-morrow is on its way.
It shall keep with its roses yet in June;
And the promise it makes perchance too soon,
For the ages fret not over a day,

THE WORLD OF PRINT AND THE WORLD'S WORK[1]

I

TURNING for a text to Victor Hugo's stirring epic of Paris, these words may be found in the section for May, and in the third chapter thereof:

"A Library implies an act of faith
Which generations still in darkness hid
Sign in their night, in witness of the dawn."

When Johann Gutenberg in his secret workshop poured the molten metal into the rough matrices he had cut for separate types, the instrument for the spread of democracy was created. When early Cavaliers and Puritans planted the crude beginnings of free public schools, the forces of democracy were multiplied. When half a century ago the first meager beginnings of the public library movement were evolved, democracy was for all time assured. Thus have three great stages, separated each by a span of two hundred years from that preceding, marked that world development whose ultimate meaning is not equality of station or possession, but equality of opportunity.

Not without stress and strife have these yet fragmentary results been achieved. Not without travail

[1] President's address at Kaaterskill Conference, American Library Association, June, 1913.

and difficulties will universal acceptance be accorded in the days to come. But no one may doubt the final outcome which shall crown the struggle of the centuries. The world was old when typography was invented. Less than five centuries have passed since then, and in this interval—but a brief period in the long history of human endeavor—there has been more enlargement of opportunity for the average man and woman than in all the time that went before. Without the instrumentality of the printed page, without the reproductive processes that give to all the world in myriad tongues the thought of all the centuries, slavery, serfdom and feudalism would still shackle the millions not so fortunate as to be born to purple and ermine, and fine linen.

II

The evolution of the book is therefore the history of the unfoldment of human rights. The chained tome in its medieval prison cell has been supplanted by the handy volume freely sent from the hospitable public library to the homes of the common people. The humblest citizen, today, has at his command books in number and in kind which royal treasuries could not have purchased five hundred years ago. In the sixteenth century, it took a flock of sheep to furnish the vellum for one edition of a book, and the product was for the very few; in the twentieth, a forest is felled to supply the paper for an edition, and the output goes to many hundred thousand readers. As books have multiplied, learning has been more widely disseminated. As more people have become educated, the demand for books has increased enormously. The multiplication of books has stimulated the writing of them, and the inevitable result has been a deterioration of quality proportioned to the increase in quantity. In the English language alone, since 1880, 206,905 titles of books printed in the United States have been listed, and 226,365 in Great Britain since 1882. Of these 433,270 titles, 84,722 represent novels—36,607 issued in the United States and 48,115 in Great Britain. Despite the inclusion of the trivial and the unsound in this vast mass of printed stuff, no one can doubt the magnitude of the service performed in the advancement of human kind. The universities have felt the touch of popular demand, and in this country at least some of them have attempted to respond. Through correspondence courses, short courses, university week conferences, summer schools, local forums, traveling instructors, and other media of extension, many institutions of higher learning have given recognition to the appeal of the masses. Logically with this enlargement of educational opportunity, the amplification of library facilities has kept pace. The libraries have become in a real sense the laboratory of learning. Intended primarily as great storehouses for the accumulation and preservation rather than the use of manuscripts and books, their doors have been opened wide to all farers in search of truth or mental stimulus.

In a report to the English King, Sir William Berkeley wrote as governor of Virginia in 1671: "I thank God there are no free schools nor printing, and I hope we shall not have them these hundred years; for learning has brought disobedience into the world, and printing has divulged them, and libels against the best government. God keep us from both."

Governor Berkeley's sentiments, expressed by him in turgid rhetoric, were held in his day by most men in authority, but that did not prevent the planting of little schoolhouses here and there, and men of much vision and little property bequeathed their possessions for maintaining them. Many a school had its origin in a bequest comprising a few milch kine, a horse or two, or a crop of tobacco; in some instances, slaves. From such beginnings, with such endowments, was evolved three hundred years ago the public system of education which today prodigally promises, though it but niggardly realizes, sixteen years of schooling for every boy and girl in the land.

If the span of years needed for the development of the free library system has been much shorter, the hostile attitude of influential men and the privations that attended pioneer efforts were no less marked. As recently as 1889 the writer of an article in the *North American Review* labeled his attack: "Are public libraries public blessings?" and answered his own question in no uncertain negative. "Not only have the public libraries, as a whole, failed to reach their proper aim of giving the means of education to the people," he protested, "but they have gone aside from their true path to furnish amusement, and that in part of a pernicious character, chiefly to the young." And he added: "I might have mentioned other possible dangers, such as the power of the directors of any library to make it a propaganda of any delusive *ism* or doctrine subversive of morality, society or government; but I prefer to rest my case here."

And it was somewhat later than this that the pages of the *Century* gave space to correspondence in opposition to the establishment of a public library system for the city of New York.

These were but echoes of earlier antagonisms.

III

For the documentary material dealing with the beginnings of the public library movement, the searcher must delve within the thousand pages of a portly folio volume issued by the British government sixty years ago. If one possesses patience sufficient to read the immense mass of dry evidence compiled by a parliamentary commission and "presented to both houses of parliament by command of Her Majesty," some interesting facts in library history will be found. A young man of twenty-three, then an underling in the service of the British Museum, afterwards an eminent librarian, was one of the principal witnesses. Edward Edwards had the gift of vision. Half a century before public libraries became the people's universities, as they are today, his prophetic tongue gave utterance to what has since become the keynote of library aims and policies. Badgered by hostile inquisitors, ridiculed by press and politicians, he undeviatingly clung to his views, and he lived to see his prophecy realized.

Great libraries there had been before his day; remarkable as a storehouse of knowledge in printed form was, and is in our own day, the institution with which he was associated. But in these rich reference collections intended for the student of research, the element of popular use was lacking. To have suggested the loan of a single book for use outside the four walls of the library would have startled and benumbed everyone in authority—and without authority—from the members of the governing board to librarian, sublibrarians, and messenger boys. This stripling faced the members of parliament, and without hesitation proclaimed his thesis.

"It is not merely to open the library to persons who, from the engrossing nature of their engagements of business, are at present utterly excluded from it, but it is also that the library may be made a direct agent in some degree in the work of national education. Let not anyone be alarmed lest something very theoretical or very revolutionary should be proposed. I merely suggest that the library should be opened to a class of men quite shut out from it by its present regulations."

Then he added: "In such a country as this, there should be one great national storehouse. But in addition to this, there should be libraries in different quarters on a humbler scale, very freely accessible."

One of the ablest members of parliament, William Ewart, of Liverpool, became intensely interested in the views expressed by young Edwards, and from that day was counted the consistent champion of library privileges for the common people. Largely through his instrumentality, aided by such men as Richard Cobden, John Bright and Joseph Brotherton, parliament passed an act "for the encouragement of museums." Out of this measure grew the later Public Libraries Act. This notable step was not accomplished without bitter opposition.

"The next thing we will be asked to do," said one indignant member on the floor of the House, "is to furnish people with quoits and peg-tops and footballs at the expense of taxpayers. Soon we will be thinking of introducing the performances of Punch for the amusement of the people."

Events in England influenced similar movements in the United States. In a letter to Edward Everett, in 1851, Mr. George Ticknor gave the first impetus to the establishment of a free public library in Boston —the first in the new world to be maintained permanently by the people for the people.

"I would establish a library which differs from all free libraries yet attempted," he wrote. "I mean one in which any popular books, tending to moral and intellectual improvement, shall be furnished in such numbers of copies that many persons can be reading the same book at the same time; in short, that not only the best books of all sorts, but the pleasant literature of the day, shall be made accessible to the whole people when they most care for it; that is, when it is new and fresh."

Sixty years after the date of Mr. Ticknor's letter, and chiefly within the last two decades of the period, the public library movement has assumed a place in public education which, relatively, the public school movement attained only after three hundred years of effort. When Thomas Bodley died, in 1613, in all Europe there were but three libraries accessible to the public—the Bodleian, the Angelo Rocca at Rome and the Ambrosian at Milan. In 1841 the Penny Cyclopedia devoted about four inches of a narrow column to the subject of libraries, ancient and modern, and limited its reference to American libraries to one sentence, obtained at second hand from an older contemporary.

"In the United States of America, according to the Encyclopedia Americana, the principal libraries are, or were in 1831, that of Harvard College, containing 36,000 volumes; the Philadelphia Library, containing 27,000; that of the Boston Athenaeum, containing 26,000; that of Congress, containing 16,000, and that of Charleston, containing 13,000."

It is only since 1867 that the federal government has deemed it worth while to compile library statistics, and the first comprehensive figures were gathered in 1875. It is worth noting that then they embraced all libraries comprising 300 volumes, and that in 1893 no mention is made of collections containing less than a thousand volumes, while the most recent official enumeration makes 5,000 volumes the unit of consideration. From these official figures may be gleaned something of the extraordinary growth of libraries, both numerically and in size. In 1875, including school libraries, there were 2,039 containing a thousand volumes, ten years later there were 4,026, ten years after that 8,000, and at this date there are in this class not less than 12,000, while the recorded number comprising three hundred volumes or more reaches the substantial total of 15,634, and 2,298 of these catalog in excess of 5,000 volumes each.

IV

These figures show phenomenal growth, but even more impressive are the facts that give their full meaning in detail. From a striking compilation issued in Germany by Die Brücke a few weeks ago, together with figures extracted by means of a questionnaire, supplemented by statistical material gathered by the Bureau of Education, the facts which follow have been deduced: Counting the great libraries of the world, the six continents abutting the seven seas possess 324 libraries whose book collections number in excess of 100,000 volumes each, and of these 79—or approximately one-fourth—are located in the Americas. Of the 79 American libraries 72 are in the United States, including university, public, governmental and miscellaneous institutions, with a combined collection of 19,295,000 volumes. If this statistical inquiry is pursued further, a reason becomes apparent why millions are starved for want of books while other millions seemingly have a surfeit of them. The rural regions, save in a handful of commonwealths whose library commissions or state libraries actively administer traveling libraries, the book supply is practically negligible. Even the hundreds of itinerating libraries but meagerly meet the want. All the traveling libraries in all the United States have a total issue annually less than that of any one twenty municipal systems that can be named. The public library facilities in at least six thousand of the smaller towns are pitifully insufficient and in hundreds of them wholly absent. The movement to supply books to the people was first launched in the rural regions seventy years ago. Indeed, the movement for popular education known as the American Lyceum, which forecast the activities of the modern public library just as the mechanics' institutes of Great Britain prepared the soil for them in that country, flourished chiefly in the less thickly settled centers of population. The early district school libraries melted away in New York state and Wisconsin and other states, and the devastated shelves have never been amply renewed. The library commissions are valiantly and energetically endeavoring to supply the want, but their efforts are all too feebly supported by their respective states. In this particular, the policy is that which unfortunately obtains as to all educational effort. More than 55 per cent of the young people from 6 to 20 years old—about 17,000,000 of them—live in the country or in towns of less than two thousand inhabitants. According to an official report from which this statement is extracted, there are 5,000 country schools still taught in primitive log houses, uncomfortable, unsuitable, unventilated, unsanitary, illy equipped, poorly lighted, imperfectly heated—boys and girls in all stages of advancement receiving instruction from one teacher of very low grade. It is plain why, in the summing up of this report, "illiteracy in rural territory is twice as great as in urban territory, notwithstanding that thousands of illiterate immigrants are crowded in the great manufacturing and industrial centers. The illiteracy among native-born children of native parentage is more than three times as great as among native children of foreign parentage, largely on account of the lack of opportunities for education in rural America." In Indian legend Nokomis, the earth, symbolizes the strength of motherhood; it may yet chance that the classic myth of the hero who gained his strength because he kissed the earth may be fully understood in America only when the people learn that they will remain strong, as Mr. Münsterberg has put it, "only by returning with every generation to the soil."

If the states have proved recreant to duty in this particular, the municipalities have shown an increasing conception of educational values. The figures make an imposing statistical array. In the United States there are 1,222 incorporated places of 5,000 or more inhabitants, and their libraries house 90,000,000 volumes, with a total yearly use aggregating 110,000,000 issues. Four million volumes a year are added to their shelves, and collectively they derive an income of $20,000,000. Their permanent endowments, which it must be regretfully said but 600 of them share, now aggregate $40,000,000. Nearly all of these libraries occupy buildings of their own, Mr. Andrew Carnegie having supplied approximately $42,226,338 for the purpose in the United States, and the balance of the $100,000,000 represented in buildings having been donated by local benefactors or raised by taxation.

The population of these 1,222 places is 38,758,584, considerably less than half that of the entire United

States. Their book possessions, on the other hand, are nine times as great as those in the rest of the country; the circulation of the books nearly twelve times in volume. Closer analysis of these figures enforces still more strongly the actual concentration of the available book supply. The hundred largest cities of the United States, varying in size from a minimum of 53,684 to a maximum of 4,766,883, possess in the aggregate more books than all the rest of the country together, and represent the bulk of the trained professional service rendered. The great majority of the 3,000 graduates whom the library schools have sent into service since the first class was organized in 1887, are in these libraries and in the university libraries. Forty per cent of the books circulated are issued to the dwellers in these one hundred cities, and in fifteen of them the stupendous total of 30,000,834 issues for home reading was recorded last year. Without such analysis as this, the statistical totals would be misleading. The concentration of resources and of trained service in large centers of population, comparatively few in number, makes evident the underlying cause for the modern trend of library development. A further study of conditions in these human hives justifies the specialized forms of service which have become a marked factor in library extension within a decade. With increased resources, with vastly improved internal machinery, with enlarged conception of opportunity for useful service, have come greater liberality of rules and ever widening circles of activity, until today no individual and no group of individuals, remains outside the radius of library influence. If this awakened zeal has spurred to efforts that seem outside the legitimate sphere of library work, no undue concern need be felt. Neither the genius and enthusiasm of the individual nor the enterprise of a group of individuals will ever be permitted to go too rapidly or too far: the world's natural conservatism and inherited unbelief stand ever ready to retard or prevent.

V

Specialization has been incorporated into library administration chiefly to give expeditious and thorough aid to seekers of information touching a wide variety of interests—business men, legislators, craftsmen, special investigators and students of every sort. This added duty has not diminished its initial function to make available the literature of all time, nor to satisfy those who go to books for the pure joy of reading. The recreative service of the library is as important as the educative, or the informative. For the great mass of people, the problem has been the problem of toil long and uninterrupted. The successful struggle of the unions to restrict the hours of labor has developed another problem almost as serious—the problem of leisure. Interwoven with this acute problem is another which subdivision of labor has introduced into modern industrial occupations—the terrible fatigue which results from a monotonous repetition of the same process hour after hour, day after day, week after week. Such blind concentration in the making of but one piece of a machine, or a garment, or a watch, or any other article of merchandise, without knowledge of its relationship to the rest, soon wears the human worker out. There must be an outlet of play, of fun, or recreation. The librarian need not feel apologetic to the public because perchance his circulation statistics show that 70 per cent of it is classed as fiction. If he wishes to reduce this percentage to 69 or 68 or 61, let him do it not by discouraging the reading of novels, but by stimulating the use of books in other classes of literature. But well does he merit his own sense of humiliation and the condemnation of the critics if he needs must feel ashamed of the kind of novels that he puts upon his shelves. To quote a fellow librarian who expresses admirably the value of such literature, "A good story has created many an oasis in many an otherwise arid life. Many-sidedness of interest makes for good morals, and millions of our fellows step through the pages of a story book into a broader world than their nature and their circumstances ever permit them to visit. If anything is to stay the narrowing and hardening process which specialization of learning, specialization of inquiry and of industry, and swift accumulation of wealth are setting up among us, it is a return to romance, poetry, imagination, fancy, and the general culture we are now taught to despise. Of all these the novel is a part; rather, in the novel are all of these. But a race may surely find springing up in itself a fresh love of romance, in the high sense of that word, which can keep it active, hopeful, ardent, progressive. Perhaps the novel is to be, in the next decades, part of the outward manifestation of a new birth of this love of breadth and happiness."

VI

Many of the factory workers are young men and young women, whose starved imaginations seek an outlet that will not be denied. In lieu of wholesome recreation and material, they will find "clues to life's perplexities" in salacious plays, in cheap vaudeville performances, in the suggestive pages of railway literature, in other ways that make for a lowering of moral tone. The reaction that craves amusement of any sort is manifest in the nightly crowded stalls of the cheap theaters. Eight million spectators view every moving picture film that is manufactured. It is estimated that one-sixth of the entire population of New York City and of Chicago attends the theaters on any Sunday of the year. One Sunday evening, at the instance of Miss Jane Addams, an investigation was made of 466 theaters in the latter city, and it was discovered that in the majority of them the leading theme was revenge; the lover following his rival; the outraged husband seeking his wife's betrayer; or the wiping out by death of a blot on a hitherto unstained honor. And of course these influences extend to the children who are always the most ardent and responsive of audiences. There is grave danger that the race will develop a ragtime disposition, a moving picture habit and a comic supplement mind.

VII

It is perhaps too early to point to the specialized attention which libraries have given to the needs of young people as a distinct contribution to society. Another generation must come before material evidence for good or ill becomes apparent. That the work is well worth the thought bestowed, whether present methods survive or are modified, may not be gainsaid. The derelicts of humanity are the wrecks who knew no guiding light. The reformatories and the workhouses, the penal institutions generally and the charitable ones principally, are not merely a burden upon society, but a reproach for duty unperformed. Society is at last beginning to realize that it is better to perfect machinery of production than to mend the imperfect product; that to dispense charity may ameliorate individual suffering, but does not prevent recurrence. And so more attention is being given prevention than cure.

"I gave a beggar from my little store
 Of well-earned gold. He spent the shining ore
 And came again, and yet again, still cold
  And hungry as before.

I gave a thought, and through that thought of mine,
He found himself a man, supreme, divine,
Bold, clothed, and crowned with blessings manifold,
 And now he begs no more."

VIII

If numbers and social and industrial importance warrant special library facilities for children, certainly the same reasons underlie the special library work with foreigners which has within recent years been carried on extensively in the larger cities. Last month the census bureau issued an abstract of startling import to those who view in the coming of vast numbers from across the waters a menace to the institutions of this democracy. According to this official enumeration, in but fourteen of fifty cities having over 100,000 inhabitants in 1910 did native whites of native parentage contribute as much as one-half the total population. The proportion exceeded three-fifths in only four cities. On the other hand, in twenty-two cities of this class, of which fifteen are in New England and the Middle Atlantic divisions, less than one-third of the population were native whites of native parentage, over two-thirds in all but one of these cities consisting of foreign-born whites and their children.

In his Ode delivered at Harvard, Lowell eloquently referred to

"The pith and marrow of a Nation
Drawing force from all her men,
Highest, humblest, weakest, all,
For her time of need, and then
Pulsing it again through them,
She that lifts up the manhood of the poor,
She of the open soul and open door,
With room about her hearth for all mankind!"

This was written in 1865. Since then the rim of the Mediterranean has sent its enormous contribution of unskilled and unlettered human beings to the New World. There have been three great tides of migration from overseas. The first came to secure liberty of conscience; the second sought liberty of political thought and action; the third came in quest of bread. And of the three, incomparably the greater problem of assimilation is that presented by the last comers. Inextricably interwoven are all the complexities which face the great and growing municipalities, politically and industrially and socially. These are the awful problems of congestion and festering slums, of corruption in public life, of the exploitation of womanhood, of terrible struggle with wretchedness and poverty. Rightly directed, the native qualities and strength of these peoples will bring a splendid contribution in the making of a virile citizenship. Wrongly shaped, their course in the life of the city may readily become of sinister import. Frequently they are misunderstood, and they easily misunderstand. The problem is one of education, but it is that most difficult problem, of education for grown-ups. Here perhaps the library may render the most distinct service, in that it can bring to them in their own tongues the ideals and the underlying principles of life and custom in their adopted country; and through their children, as they swarm into the children's rooms, is established a point of contact which no other agency could so effectually provide.

Under the repressive measures of old-world governments, the racial culture and national spirit of Poles, Lithuanians, Finns, Balkan Slavs, and Russian Jews have been stunted. Here both are warmed into life and renewed vigor, and in generous measure are given back to the land of their adoption. Such racial contribution must prove of enormous value, whether, as many sociologists believe, this country is to prove a great melting pot for the fusing of many races, or whether as Dr. Zhitlowsky contends, there is to be one country, one set of laws, one speech, but a vast variety of national cultures, contributing each its due share to the enrichment of the common stock.

IX

Great changes have come about in the methods that obtain for the exercise of popular government. In a democracy whose chief strength is derived from an intelligent public opinion, the sharpening of such intelligence and enlargement of general knowledge concerning affairs of common concern are of paramount importance. Statute books are heavily cumbered with laws that are unenforced because public opinion goes counter to them. Nonenforcement breeds disrespect for law, and unscientific making of laws leads to their disregard. So the earliest attempts to find a remedy contemplated merely the legislator and the official, bringing together for their use through the combined services of trained economists and of expert reference librarians the principles and foundation for contemplated legislation and the data as to similar attempts elsewhere. Fruitful as this service has proved within the limitation of state and municipal officialdom, a broadened conception of possibilities now enlarges the scope of the work to include citizen organizations interested in the study of public questions, students of sociology, economics and political science, business men keenly alive to the intimate association—in a legitimate sense—of business and politics, and that new and powerful element in public affairs which has added three million voters to the poll lists in ten states, and will soon add eleven million voters more in the remaining thirty-eight. The new library service centering in state and municipal legislative reference libraries, and in civic departments of large public libraries, forecasts the era, now rapidly approaching, when aldermen and state representatives will still enact laws and state and city officials will enforce them, but their making will be determined strictly by public opinion. The local government of the future will be by quasi-public citizen organizations directing aldermen and state legislators accurately to register their will. When representative government becomes misrepresentative, in the words of a modern humorist, democracy will ask the Powers that Be whether they are the Powers that Ought to Be. To intelligently determine the answer, public opinion must not ignorantly ask.

X

This has been called the age of utilitarianism. Such it unquestionably is, but its practicality is not disassociated from idealism. The resources of numberless commercial enterprises are each in this day reckoned in millions, and their products are figured in terms of many millions more, as once thousands represented the spread of even the greatest of industries. But more and more business men are coming to realize that business organization as it affects for weal or woe thousands who contribute to their success, must be conducted as a trust for the common good, and not merely for selfish exploitation, or for oppression. As the trade guilds of old wielded their vast power for common ends, so all the workers gave the best at their command to make their articles of merchandise the most perfect that human skill and care could produce. Men of business whose executive skill determines the destinies of thousands in their employ, are growing more and more to an appreciation of the trusteeship that is theirs. A humane spirit is entering the relationship between employer and employed. Great commercial organizations are conducting elaborate investigations into conditions of housing, sanitation, prolongation of school life, social insurance and similar subjects of betterment for the toilers; but a brief span ago they were concerned chiefly with trade extension and lowering of wages, all unconcerned about the living conditions of their dependents. They too are now exemplifying the possession of that constructive imagination which builds large and beyond the present. For results that grow out of experience and of experiment they also are in part dependent upon the sifted facts that are found in print. The business house library is a recent development, and in ministering in different ways to both employer and employed, gives promise of widespread usefulness.

XI

With the tremendous recent growth of industrialism and the rapid multiplication of invention, the manifest need for making available the vast sum of gathered knowledge concerning the discoveries of modern science has evolved the great special libraries devoted to the varied subdivisions of the subject. Munificently endowed as many of them are, highly organized for ready access to material, administered to encourage use and to give expert aid as well, their great importance cannot be overestimated. What they accomplish is not wholly reducible to statistics, nor can their influence be readily traced, perhaps, to the great undertakings of today which overshadow the seven wonders of antiquity. But there can be no question that without the opportunities that here lie for study and research, and—no less important—without the skilled assistance freely rendered by librarian and bibliographer, special talent would often remain dormant and its possessor unsatisfied. Greater here would be the loss to society than to the individual.

XII

Thus the libraries are endeavoring to make themselves useful in every field of human enterprise or interest; with books of facts for the information they possess; with books of inspiration for the stimulus they give and the power they generate. Conjointly these yield the equipment which develops the constructive imagination, without which the world would seem but a sorry and a shriveled spot to dwell upon. The poet and the dreamer conceive the great things which are wrought; the scientist and the craftsman achieve them; the scholar and the artist interpret them. Thus associated, they make their finest contribution to the common life. The builders construct the great monuments of iron and of concrete which are the expression of this age, as the great cathedrals and abbeys were of generations that have passed. Adapted as they are to the needs of this day, our artists and our writers have shown us the beauty and the art which the modern handiwork of man possesses. With etcher's tool one man of keen insight has shown us the art that inheres in the lofty structures which line the great thoroughfares of our chief cities, the beauty of the skylines they trace with roof and pediment. With burning words another has given voice to machinery and to the vehicles of modern industry, and we thrill to the eloquence and glow of his poetic fervor.

"Great works of art are useful works greatly done," declares Dr. T. J. Cobden-Sanderson, and, rightly viewed, the most prosaic achievements of this age, whether they be great canals or clusters of workmen's homes worthily built, or maybe more humble projects, have a greatness of meaning that carries with it the sense of beauty and of art.

In medieval days, the heralds of civilization were the warrior, the missionary, the explorer and the troubadour; in modern times, civilization is carried forward by the chemist, the engineer, the captain of industry, and the interpreter of life—whether the medium utilized be pen or brush or voice. Without vision, civilization would wither and perish, and so it may well be that the printed page shall serve as symbol of its supreme vision. Within the compass of the book sincerely written, rightly chosen, and well used are contained the three chief elements which justify the library of the people—information, education, recreation.

The urge of the world makes these demands; ours is the high privilege to respond.

LIBRARY WORK WITH CHILDREN[1]

IT IS amid conditions that call for heroic effort that the public library of today must do its work with children. There are not wanting critics who decry some present-day tendencies. They saw that when librarians seek the children in their homes to form groups of readers, they encroach upon the domain of the settlement worker. They complain that the story hour, now so widely developed, is an invasion of the kindergarten; they view with alarm the use of the stereoscope and stereopticon as being outside the legitimate domain of the institution. Perhaps they are right, and perhaps they are wrong; maybe they are both right and wrong. If the purposes sought by these means were adequately ministered to from other sources, it may well be questioned whether the library would be justified in adopting these methods. In the admitted lack of agencies to meet these conditions, the children's librarian may find satisfaction in the results obtained, even if some folks' notions of legitimate library work are sadly jolted, as in the time to come they will certainly have to be modified. At best, the library and all allied agencies are struggling against tremendous odds in counteracting subtle influences for evil and open influences that breed coarseness and vulgarity. To operate a moving-picture

[1] Extracts from a paper in the *Educational Bi-monthly,* April, 1910, entitled, "The Chicago Public Library and Co-operation with the Schools."

show within the sacred precincts of a library may be counter to the accepted view of the fitness of things, but those who have visited the children's department of the Cincinnati Public Library will recall with a glow of pleasure the sight of the interested group of children awaiting each his turn at the machine to go on a tarry-at-home journey to Switzerland and France and other countries over-sea. Would the critics prefer to have the children glue their faces to the glass in the vulgar and suggestive shows of the penny arcade? The craving for novelty and amusement will not be denied. The instinct for dramatic action is inherent. It is said that there are 5,000 penny arcades and nickelodeons in New York City alone, with an average daily attendance of 300,000 children, and scarce a hamlet in all this wide country that does not foster one or two of them, a large proportion of them supplied with pictures of doubtful propriety.

The average penny arcade is closely linked with the Sunday comic supplement and the yellow-backed pamphlet in the vulgarization and decadence that threatens to overwhelm the youth of the country. Parents who would be horrified to note in the hands of their children any specimen of dime novel literature, complacently turn over to them on Sunday morning the sheet splashed with daubs of red and yellow and green that serve to render attractive the accompanying pictures and their slangy explanations. The Sunday comic supplement has done more to debase and to brutalize what is fine in boys and girls, to debauch their sense of fairness, to blunt their ideas as to what is manly and fair, to deaden their respect for age and authority, to prevent such aesthetic sense as they may have had, than can be counteracted by all the attempts being made by school, church, museum and library to stimulate a taste for better things. There is no escape from these colored atrocities. Millions enter the households weekly, they are scattered broadcast in parks and on the streets, they are left upon the seats of railway trains and street cars—they are everywhere. Parental effort is powerless. In a few households they are ruthlessly barred, but the neighbors' children are willing to share without demur. In an address before the American Playgrounds Congress, recently held in New York City, Miss Maud Summers uttered a warning against this pernicious fostering of deceit, cunning, and disrespect for age.

"The child of sensible parents will not see or know about them," Mr. Lindsay Swift wrote in a contribution to *The Printing Art* two years ago, "but the child of the street, the child of the indifferent household, will warm to them like a cat to the back of the stove. There are certain negative results that parents have a right to expect from every educative force which is brought to bear on their children; that these children shall not be deliberately taught disrespect for old age or for physical infirmities and deformities; that they shall not learn to cherish contempt for other races or religions than their own; that they shall not take satisfaction in the tormenting of animals or weaklings—in short, that they shall not acquire an habitually cynical and unsportsmanlike attitude of mind. A morbid gloating over the deficiencies and humiliations of our neighbors is pretty sure to develop vulgarity and a lax moral fibre in ourselves; for vulgarity of mind and manners seems to me to be primarily a lack of restraint in thought, feeling, and expression regarding those tendencies which every civilized man and race is striving to modify or to conquer."

Doubtless, when first this medium for purveying humor was devised, the tendencies now so apparent were minimized. There were, in some of the earlier attempts, real humor and some skill of pencil, but the pictures have degenerated until they cry aloud for suppression.

There need be no apology for the story hour. A good story well told makes for pleasure, makes for morals, makes for intellectual growth. Most librarians defend it on the ground that the telling of the story leads to the reading of books on related topics. To my mind, no such defense or even explanation is needed. The story, if well chosen and fittingly told, justifies the teller and the tale. It is a moot question in educational circles whether the ear is a better medium for receiving impressions than is the eye. Some school-masters aver that there are ear-minded children and there are eye-minded children. A good story, well told, is worthy of being counted in the circulation statistics as many times as there are children to hear it, and far worthier to so figure than many a book that is taken out on a card and leaves as faint and as durable an impression on the reader's mind as footsteps on the shifting sand. And the more the storyteller can lead back the mind of childhood to the heart of childhood, the tales of wonder and of myth that grew to fulness when the race was young, the greater the service and the more fruitful in giving the listener something that will endure.

Neither is there need for apology in the exploitation of home library groups. At best, these can but partially counteract the flood of cheap and decadent literature of the most depraved character that circulates secretly among boys and girls. In Buffalo, recently, the public library has found among the people of foreign birth a mass of material in circulation whose bad quality has surprised even the librarians. The home groups that are being formed in some of the larger cities find an opening wedge among people of foreign birth whose reading has been practically confined to stuff of this sort. The reports from Germany would hardly seem credible were they not vouched for by the Durer Union, whose campaign against the growing tendency to read trashy literature has unearthed these facts. In a statement issued by its secretary, the astounding declaration is made that 8,000 established booksellers and 30,000 peddlers were engaged in selling sensational serials and books containing complete tales of a very low order.

No fewer than 750,000 of these wretched stories have been sold in the course of a single year. They are hawked from house to house, from factory to factory, outside schools, and among the peasants on every farm throughout the empire. The peddlers nearly always enter by the back door or the kitchen stairs. Servant girls and ignorant peasantry are the most fruitful customers, but it is asserted by municipal officials that even people who are in receipt of poor relief often deprive themselves of necessities in order to save two cents for a vile rehash of the sensationally embellished details of a notorious crime.

The extent of the literature of the streets obtainable in this country is little appreciated. An investigation, instituted several years ago by the Library Commission of one of the Middle West states, demonstrated the existence of tons of it on the upper and back-row shelves of news stands in all the larger cities, and in many of the villages and hamlets as well.

The desire to show a large circulation has made many librarians yield to the tyranny of statistics, and some errors of library administration are attributable to this cause. While it is undoubtedly true that the chief function of the library is to distribute as many wholesome books as possible, among the people, the totals of circulation are of vastly inferior importance to some facts that are not susceptible of being arranged in statistical uniform. And this is more particularly true of children's reading. It is less a question of how many books are read than what books are read and by whom they are read. It may well be urged that there is greater importance in the quality of the circulation than in the size of it—not how many, but how good, should be the earnest inquiry. It may well de doubted whether some children do not read more books than they can well assimilate. They are mentally profited about as much as their physical condition is nourished when they quaff quantities of soda water. They become troubled with mental dyspepsia.

Another criticism that is pertinent applies to book selection. There are too many books written especially for children. There are more titles in the average collection of children's books than the librarian ought to purchase. There are too many books that are negative in quality—pleasantly enough flavored, not harmful in tone, authentic as to facts, but colorless. There are usually too few of the world's enduring books—classics—and too many editions edited especially for children. Some of the children's catalogues are of appalling size. Here there is abundant need of excision. Five hundred titles, judiciously chosen and plentifully duplicated, would meet the need of most libraries, and would immeasurably raise the standard of reading. Much might be ascertained by an analysis of the individual cards of juvenile patrons—a sort of laboratory experiment.

There is need for greater co-operation between teachers and librarians. There are tendencies in teaching that are strangling rather than imparting the love of fine literature. It is no longer sufficient to give to the reader the music of lyric, the stir of epic—poetry must serve as an exercise in grammar. It is not sufficient that from virile prose the reader may obtain the glow of the writer's fancy or thought—it must do duty as a bit of sentence construction, or a companion piece to a lesson in geography or, perhaps, of history. We are told that poetry is dead. Who killed it? and how long would it take to do the like for prose?

Whatever of criticism as to plan and method may be rightfully made against public library work with children, the earnestness that underlies it all will, in the end, serve to eliminate the real causes for such criticism. Its meaning will unfold as time goes on—the first children's room opened in a public library dates back not much more than a dozen years. In the almonry of Westminster, three and one-half centuries ago, William Caxton chose carefully for his printing press, with deep reverence in his heart for the white souls upon which his characters would be printed as surely as upon the white paper before him. And with that same thought and care will be sifted, in the work that is being carried on now, the printed page that helps to mould and build the character of the newer generations.

TRAVELLING LIBRARIES[1]

FOLLOWING in the wake of the great public library movement, which in less than two decades has dotted the cities of the United States with buildings that house millions of books for the people, came systems of traveling libraries. The institutions which Jenkin Lloyd Jones satirically terms Carnegeries, provide city dwellers with an amplitude of reading material, but there was until a few years ago no provision for similarly meeting the greater needs of the isolated persons living remote from centers of population—in thousands of little hamlets, in mining and lumber camps, in uncounted farmhouses.

Just fifteen years ago, Mr. Melvil Dewey, then state librarian of New York, ever foremost in progressive library work and originator of most of the far-reaching methods for making public libraries useful and efficient, solved the problem which had bothered many thinkers on the subject: How to give country people access to collections of books selected by experienced and educated buyers, and how to renew these collections so as to keep a fresh and plentiful supply on hand at all times. Mr. Dewey's solution of the problem was absurdly simple. Anybody could have thought it out without effort—but nobody else did. It was this: From a centrally administered

[1] Extracts from booklet, *"Books for the People,"* 1908.

library, groups of books carefully selected so as to comprise fifty or sixty volumes each, were packed into suitable boxes or cases, and sent to small villages, country schoolhouses, and centrally located farmhouses, to be distributed to the neighborhoods on the same plan as books are given out from branch stations in cities. At the end of six months, the books would be gathered by the custodian, shipped back to the central distributing agency, and a fresh lot would take their place. By this simple and economical method the people of these little neighborhoods would secure an opportunity to read the best and most interesting books without financial burden.

"In the work of popular education," said Melvil Dewey pertinently, "it is, after all, not the few great libraries, but the thousand small that may do most for the people."

In fifteen years, the first little chest of books that went upon its travels has multiplied to more than 5,000. Probably a third of a million books are now constantly "on the go" in this fashion. Figures are available for only twenty-two of the states, and according to these the circulation for the states enumerated was 600,443 books last year. It must be remembered that for a few years after the plan was transplanted from New York to other states, private contributions were the only reliance for maintaining the systems of traveling libraries. It is only within the last half dozen years that the demonstration of their usefulness prompted state legislatures to make appropriations for this purpose, to enable state library commissions to extend this great work on a liberal scale. The ease with which the traveling libraries may be adapted to meet various needs may be shown in a rapid summary compiled by Mr. F. A. Hutchins, who has been one of the leading promoters of them in this state.

Some women in New Jersey have used them to lighten the long winter days and evenings of the brave men who belong to the life-saving service, and that state has now taken up the traveling library as a definite part of the work of its state library; other women, in Salt Lake City, send them regularly to remote valleys in Utah; a number of state federations of women's clubs use them to furnish books for study to isolated clubs; Mrs. Eugene B. Heard of Middleton, Ga., is devoting herself to the supervision of an admirable system which reaches a large number of small villages on the Seaboard Air Line in five southern states; an association in Washington, D. C., puts libraries on the canal-boats which ply on the Washington and Potomac Canal in the summer and "tie-up" in small hamlets in the Blue Ridge Mountains in the winter; the colored graduates of Hampton Institute carry libraries to the schools for their own people at the base of the Cumberland Mountains, while to the "mountain whites" libraries are sent by women's clubs in Kentucky, Tennessee, and Alabama. In Idaho, California, Nebraska, Kansas, Illinois, Missouri, Minnesota, and many other states, women's clubs are doing the same work for miners, lumbermen, farmers, and sailors. The people of British Columbia and New Zealand are successfully imitating their American cousins in this work. In Massachusetts, where nearly every community has its public library, the Woman's Educational Association is doing a most helpful work by using traveling libraries to strengthen the weak public libraries in the hill towns.

Of all the states of the Union which reported on traveling libraries last year, Wisconsin stood first with a circulation of 122,093. Wisconsin was the third state to adopt this method for bringing wholesome books to people in the country. This was in 1895. The Free Library Commission has charge of 563 of these little libraries, which are sent to stations scattered all over the state and are exchanged every six months. Each group contains books of history, travel, fiction, biography, useful arts, and miscellaneous literature so proportioned as to meet the needs of the average community as determined by experience. The Wisconsin Commission also sends to communities where there are many persons of foreign birth, the best literature in their own tongues. In some sections of the state, people go ten to twenty miles at regular intervals to secure these books. The Commission also makes up study libraries for the use of clubs engaged in serious study. The topics deal with English literature, art, history, village and town improvement, questions of the day, etc.

II

Fifteen years ago there existed within the fifty-six thousand square miles of Wisconsin a mere handful of starveling public libraries, and only in three or four of the larger cities were these institutions properly housed. Most of them existed from force of habit rather than from action. But one library in the state employed trained service. There were no traveling libraries. The school district libraries had scarcely made a beginning, so that even that source failed to supply wholesome books for the use of the people. Here and there a volunteer fire department gathered a bundle of books, or a literary society would secure a similar collection from the attics of its members. Naturally, such efforts resulted in dismal failures. Ninety per cent of the population was absolutely without public library facilities.

But fifteen years ago, and now! Scattered all over the state, in cities and villages and hamlets, are to be found modern, up-to-date public libraries in charge of alert, trained, interested librarians, eager and active in extending the radius of their influence or helpful in every way to promote the interests of the community and of every individual in it. There are now 152 public libraries in Wisconsin. Sixty-one of them occupy buildings erected especially for them, and 28 others have quarters in city halls or other public buildings. Many of them have a children's department, with trained library workers in charge of the specialized activities there conducted. In the larger buildings, lecture halls are an adjunct, where it is possible to provide university extension and similar lectures, and where women's study clubs, young men's debating societies and similar groups of persons find hospitable meeting places for carrying on their work. Work with schools is carried on to an extent, and to a profitable degree, little imagined as possible in the early days of the library extension movement. Free access to shelves is now permitted in every library of the state except one.

There are now some forty librarians in Wisconsin who come from library training schools, and of the other librarians and assistants employed, approximately 100 have attended the summer school conducted by the Wisconsin Free Library Commission. The growing importance of the relation between library and school is evidenced by the fact that library instruction is now part of the course in every one of the seven normal schools, and a professional school for training librarians, with a staff of picked instructors, is maintained at Madison by the state. The candidates for admission are selected by competitive examination, and with special regard to suitability for the work by reason of temperament, education, address and experience.

III

Naturally, the activity of the public library movement in recent years, with consequent multiplication of institutions, has attracted the attention of thoughtful men and enlisted the cordial aid of public-spirited individuals. Philanthropists have found therein an avenue for their benefactions yielding undoubted results. Many wealthy men, instead of rearing to their own honor shafts of stone or images in bronze, have taken the wiser and happier method of securing an enduring monument in the form of a public library. There are now living a number of wealthy men who have provided in their wills for suitable bequests whereby buildings of this character may be erected in the places which they make their home, and similarly others have provided endowments for their home libraries to come out of their estates. Thus does one good deed suggest another.

IV

The work of the Free Library Commission may be briefly summarized as follows:

Supervision. Works for the establishment of public libraries in localities able to support them.

Visits libraries for the purpose of giving advice and instruction.

Collects and publishes statistics of libraries for the guidance and information of trustees.

Prints a bi-monthly bulletin, news notes and suggestions to keep librarians and trustees informed in regard to library progress throughout the state.

Gives advice and assistance in planning library buildings and collects material on this subject for the use of library boards.

Instruction. Aids in organizing new libraries.

Assists in reorganizing old libraries according to modern methods which insure the best results and greatest efficiency of the library.

Conducts a school for library training for the purpose of improving the service in small libraries.

Holds institutes for librarians to instruct those who cannot attend summer school.

Traveling Libraries. Maintains a system of traveling libraries which furnishes books to rural communities and villages too small to support local libraries, and to larger villages and towns as an inducement to establish free public libraries.

Aids in organization and administration of county traveling library systems.

Clearing House. Operates a clearing house for magazines to build up reference collections of bound periodicals in the public libraries of the state.

Document Department. Maintains a document department for the use of state officers, members of the legislature and others interested in the growth and development of affairs in the state, and catalogues and exchanges state documents for the benefit of public libraries.

Book Lists. Distributes a suggestive list of books for small libraries to insure purchase of the books in the best editions.

Issues frequent buying lists of current books to aid committees in securing the best investment of book funds.

Compiles buying lists on special subjects or for special libraries upon request.

V

It must not be supposed, because the great library growth has been manifested in the last decade, that there were wanting prior to that period interested men and women hopeful and active to give impulse for like conditions. Away back in 1840, when Wisconsin was a frontier territory ambitious to advance to statehood, the council and assembly enacted a law to encourage subscription libraries. A public library supported by taxation was not then dreamed of, for there was then none in the entire United States, nor for ten years thereafter. It is interesting to note that in these territorial days, the little hamlet of log houses known as Madison enjoyed the advantages of a library open to all who cared to use it. It was the private library of the governor, James Duane Doty, which he threw open to the public. Col. Geo. W. Bird, in his account of it, says that it contained about five hundred volumes of a general historical, educational and literary character and a number of the best maps known at that time. It was housed in the governor's private office, which was a small one-story frame building of one room situated among the trees in the little backwoods town. The books were arranged in low shelving around the sides of the room, and the scanty furniture, consisting of a small desk, a deal-board table, three or four chairs, a pine bench, and a register in which to enter the taking and returning of books, completed the equipment.

Over the shelving on the westerly side of the room, was this direction, painted in black on a white field: "Take, Read and Return." There were only two regulations as to the use of the library and they were displayed conspicuously in red ink about the room, and they were as follows:

1. Any white resident between the lakes, the Catfish and the westerly hills, his wife and children, may have the privileges of this library so long as they do not soil or injure the books, and properly return them.

2. Any such resident, his wife or children, may take from the library one book at a time and retain it not to exceed two weeks, and then return it, and on failure to return promptly, he or she shall be considered, and published, as an outcast in the community.

"I do not remember of there ever having been occasion for inflicting this penalty. I do remember my father sending me one day when the time-limit of a book was about to expire, with a note to a family, requiring the return of a book that day, and calling attention pointedly to the above penalty of failure; and I remember how concerned the mother was, and how quickly she got the book and dragging me along after her, speedily returned it to the library, and thus escaped the sentence of outlawry," concludes Col. Bird.

VI

What is known far and wide as the Maxon bookmark originated in Wisconsin, and was the conception of the Rev. Mr. Maxon, then resident in Dunn County. It has been reprinted on little slips in hundreds of forms, has circulated in every state and territory in the country, and doubtless a full million copies of it have been slipped between the leaves of children's books. It may fittingly be reproduced here:

"Once on a time" A Library Book was overheard talking to a little boy who had just borrowed it. The words seemed worth recording and here they are:

"Please don't handle me with dirty hands. I should feel ashamed to be seen when the next little boy borrowed me.

Or leave me out in the rain. Books can catch cold as well as children.

Or make marks on me with your pen or pencil. It would spoil my looks.

Or lean on me with your elbows when you are reading me. It hurts.

Or open me and lay me face down on the table. You would not like to be treated so.

Or put in between my leaves a pencil or anything thicker than a single sheet of thin paper. It would strain my back.

Whenever you are through reading me, if you are afraid of losing your place, don't turn down the corner of one of my leaves, but have a neat little Book Mark to put in where you stopped, and then close me and lay me down on my side so that I can have a good comfortable rest."

ADMINISTRATION OF LIBRARY FUNDS[1]

JUST a few words on a matter of business addressed to business men—for that, I conceive, is what mayors and aldermen primarily are, whether engaged in trade or in professions. I am aware that it is more popular to term them politicians in the worst meaning of that abused word, and to ascribe improper motives to their official actions, but personal relations with many of them through a long series of years convinces me that a very large majority of them are men of probity and good intentions, seeking to perform a public duty to the extent of their abilities. They are sure of clamorous condemnation for any errors of commission or omission, and very uncertain of commendation for conscientious attention to official duties. Lest these remarks may be construed as undue flattery prompted by the presence here of so many municipal officers, it may be added that the average alderman is inclined to be at times a bit self-opinionated in his views of public business, or impatient with that phase of it which he does not directly control. At least this is so until his term is nearing its end. Unfortunately, the broader and wider outlook which experience always brings to men usually develops too late, except in cases of re-election, for service during his own period of administration, and cannot be transmitted to his suc-

[1] *The Municipality*, Dec., 1905.

cessor. And that is why, rather than because of downright dishonesty, our city public works are frequently defectively constructed, money is needlessly expended for certain purposes, and not expended at all, or insufficiently expended for others, where it would bring best results.

A municipality ought to be a business corporation purely, managed on business principles by its board of trustees (aldermen) and for the benefit of the stockholders (taxpayers and citizens). Like any other business institution, its management should carefully consider its resources and apportion expenditures to secure largest returns on investment. And in the case of a municipality, the returns from investments embrace both the material comforts and necessities of community life which are represented in sanitation, facilities for transportation, for lighting and for adequate water supply, and the intellectual requirements of modern life which find their expression in good public schools and well-administered libraries.

And this brings us to a consideration of the question immediately before us—the administration of public library funds. Some years ago a discussion of this question might have required a preliminary apologetic justification for the existence of such an institution as a public library. The necessity for that sort of thing has happily passed, just as the need for explanation in the reasonable expenditure of public funds for public schools is no longer existent. Nevertheless, the general conception of the possibilities of usefulness in public library work remains imperfectly developed. It will require time and patient effort to secure full recognition of the potent possibilities for the good of all the people that may be realized through the public library adequately maintained and properly administered. And herein lies the crux of the question.

That anecdote which Souther told of himself will bear repetition. Meeting an old woman one stormy day, he resorted to the usual topic of greeting: "Dreadful weather, isn't it?" he remarked.

This was quite obvious, of course, but the old woman's rejoinder was rather philosophical.

"*Any* weather is better than none," quoth she.

This philosophic way of viewing a discouraging condition is, I fear, but too true with reference to the average public library. But *any* library is not necessarily better than none. The average municipality is quite likely to rest satisfied with prevailing conditions. If municipalities were, like other business corporations, subjected to the test of competition, many of them would be in the hands of the sheriff. No business man can survive today who does not utilize modern progressive methods. The successful business man today is he who adopts the principle that no results can be secured without certain outlays. No farmer would conceive it prudent to economize in the planting of his seed. If he did, scanty crops would convince him of the error of his methods. And yet it is this error which many cities and towns commit. They may possess libraries, but they grudgingly allow them revenues just sufficient to keep them from starvation. In Wisconsin we have a goodly percentage of public libraries that are in every way creditable, but it is too true that there are also many which fail to realize their full possibilities.

In order that the maximum dividend on the investment may be realized, it is essential that a library's resources should permit:

1. The employment of competent trained service.

2. The purchase of books and magazines at frequent intervals to keep the library from going to seed.

3. Such regulations that the doors of the institution shall be open at least as often and as long every week as they are allowed to remain closed.

To effect these desiderata, the library boards should be given sufficient funds, with due regard to economy of administration. It is coming to be recognized that a librarian is expected to do more than hand out books over a counter and take them in again—that the up-to-date librarian must study the social, commercial and intellectual interests of the community so as to make the library a vital force by providing the facilities for expansion of these interests. The public schools educate the average person during an average period representing five years of his life; the public library should afford facilities to persons of every age and in every condition of life for continuing one's education indefinitely. The public officer desirous of ascertaining the best methods for paving streets, the housewife in search of receipts for the most wholesome dishes for her table, the mechanic seeking to better his condition by studying the latest improvements in his craft, the foreign-born reader anxious for literature bearing on the duties of citizenship, the young man engaged in serious study of current questions—these and every other man, woman or child in quest of information, should have the facilities offered in the public libraries to secure it fully, not only by personal search along the shelves, but through the ready, helpful and suggestive assistance of a librarian trained to find in a multitude of print the essential facts which are wanted. Individual cases could be cited by the score to demonstrate what a public library can do for the people of its community. One that came to my attention recently may be mentioned. A boy who gave promise of no virtues and many vices engendered by idleness, was the despair of his parents and the annoyance of the neighbors. By chance he wandered into the reference room of the library in his town, carelessly picked up a book dealing with inventions, became interested, came again, asked for and received more books on the same topic and studied them with increasing interest. From that day be became a changed boy. He had found a purpose in life. Today, through his own efforts, he is taking the engineering course in a college, he has secured a patent from the government for a valuable invention, and he gives promise of becoming a leader in his chosen profession. In a certain city of this state which need not be designated by name, there are large manufacturing interests. There is a public library magnificently housed, but until lately without an appropriation for keeping the book purchases up-to-date. Workmen were eager to get books on electricity, on general mechanics and useful arts effecting their daily labor, but there were no funds with which to purchase them; naturally, they soon ceased their visits to the library. When the Free Library Commission called the attention of the heads of these great industrial enterprises to the condition of affairs, they immediately saw the advantage of adequately supporting the library. It did not take them long to figure out that no cheaper method could be devised for improving the product of their establishments and to create an interest among their workmen that would make for greater industry, better workmanship and consequently increased profits. On their part the workmen were quick to see their own advantage in increased wages in proportion to increase in skill and output. As an economic proposition the net result is greater stability in the industrial life of the community—decreased labor troubles and increased confidence between employer and employed. A sociologist who made a systematic study of a group of villages largely populated by workingmen, reported that the one which showed greatest evidence of prosperity, cleanliness and attractiveness of homes generally, was one conspicuous by reason of its well-managed public library.

There is no channel of human usefulness which appeals so forcefully to the modern spirit of philanthropy as the public library. This generosity would, I doubt not, be greatly multiplied were there any assurance that the communities to be benefited would properly maintain the institution given to it. Purely as a matter of business, it pays to support a library decently. But deeper than this lies the motive that should actuate any city or town to erect within its midst an institution that must stand as the exponent of its intellectual and to some extent its social life.

"The problem before us," said Lowell many years ago, "is to make a whole of many discordant parts, our many foreign elements; and I know of no way in which this can better be done than by providing a common system of education, and a common door of access to the best books by which that education may be continued, broadened and made fruitful."

These words are as true today as when they were uttered.